RETURN TO THE CENTRE

Formerly a monk of Prinknash Abbey and Prior of Farn-borough Abbey in England, Bede Griffiths went to India in 1955 and assisted in the foundation of Kurisumala Ashram, a monastery of the Syrian rite in Kerala. In 1968 he came with two monks from Kurisumala to Saccidananda Ashram, Shantivanam, in Tamil Nadu (the former Madras State). This ashram was founded in 1950 by two Frenchmen, Jules Monchanin and Henri le Saux, and was a pioneer attempt in India to found a Christian community following the customs of a Hindu ashram and adapting itself to Hindu ways of life and thought. It seeks to become a prayer-centre, where people of different religious traditions can meet together in an atmosphere of prayer and grow together towards that unity in Truth which is the goal of all religion.

He is the author of THE GOLDEN STRING.

RETURN TO THE CENTRE

BEDE GRIFFITHS

COLLINS
Fount Paperbacks

First published 1976
by William Collins Sons & Co Ltd
First issued in Fount Paperbacks 1978
Third impression June 1984

© Bede Griffiths 1976

'For, though God be everywhere present, yet he is only present to thee in the deepest and most central part of thy soul. Thy natural senses cannot possess God or unite thee to him; nay, thy inward faculties of understanding, will, and memory, can only reach after God, but cannot be the place of his habitation in thee. But there is a root or depth in thee from whence all these faculties come forth, as lines from a centre or as branches from the body of the tree. This depth is called the Centre, the *Fund* or Bottom of the soul. This depth is the unity, the eternity, I had almost said the infinity of thy soul; for it is so infinite that nothing can satisfy it or give it any rest but the infinity of God.'

WILLIAM LAW

CONTENTS

ONE

A *Sannyasi* in India

I sit here on the veranda of my cell, watching the sun set behind the trees, and recall the day, nearly fifty years ago, when I watched the same sun setting over the playing-fields at school. My cell is a thatched hut surrounded by trees. I can listen to the birds singing, as I did then, and watch the trees making dark patterns against the sky as the light fades, but I have travelled a long way both in space and in time since then. There are tall palmyra palms around me, and young coconut trees growing up between them, and the bananas are spreading their broad leaves like green sails. I can hear a robin singing, but it is a black Indian robin, and the voice of the cuckoo which comes from the distant woods is that of the Indian cuckoo. I have made my home here in India, in the Tamil Nadu, by the banks of the river Cavery, but my mind has also travelled no less far than my body. For sixteen years now I have lived as an Indian among Indians, following Indian ways of life, studying Indian thought, and immersing myself in the living traditions of the Indian spirit. Let me now try to reflect on what India has done to me, on how my mind has developed over these years, on the changes which have taken place in my way of life and in the depths of my soul.

The first thing that I have learned is a simplicity of life which before I would have not thought possible. India has a way of reducing human needs to a minimum. One full meal a day of rice and vegetables – at best with some curds and ghee (clarified butter) – is considered sufficient. Tea or coffee with some rice preparation and some pickle is enough for breakfast and supper. Nor are tables and chairs, spoons and forks and knives and plates considered necessary. One sits on the floor on a mat and eats with one's hands – or rather with the right hand, as the left hand is kept for cleansing one's self. For plate there is a banana leaf. There is thus no need of any furniture in an Indian home. The richer people who have adopted Western ways may make use of tables and chairs and beds and other conveniences, but the poor man – and that is the vast majority – is still content to sit and sleep on the floor. Nor are elaborate bathrooms and lavatories considered necessary. In the villages the majority of people will take their bath at a pump or a well or in a neighbouring tank or stream, and most people still go out into the fields or by the roadside or by a stream to relieve themselves. There is a beautiful simplicity in all this, which makes one realize something of the original simplicity of human nature. Even clothes are hardly necessary. Most men today, it is true, wear a shirt and a 'dhoti' – a piece of cloth wound round the waist and falling to the feet – and women wear a sari and a blouse to cover the breast, but this is comparatively recent. Even now clothes are still felt to be things which are put on for the occasion, and are easily discarded. A man will take his shirt off when he wants to relax, and a labourer will wear no more than a 'langothi' – a piece of cloth wound round the middle and between the legs.

All this makes the life of a *sannyasi* – one who has 'renounced' the world – immensely simple. He needs no house or furniture. He may live in a cave or take shelter beside a temple or on the veranda of a house. For clothing he needs only two pieces of cloth – which should not be stitched – one to wear round the waist and the other for a shawl to cover the shoulders or the head. There are even some *sannyasis* who renounce all clothing and are said to be 'clothed with the sky'. For food he needs only one meal a day, which he gets by begging or, more often, which a householder will offer him unasked. He can thus reduce his life to an absolute simplicity. He is totally detached from the world, depending on divine providence for his bare needs of food, shelter and clothing. Does this not bring him very near to the first disciples of Christ, who were told to take 'no gold, nor silver, nor copper in your belts, no bag for your journey, nor two tunics, nor sandals, nor a staff', and to the Son of man himself, who had nowhere to lay his head?[1] What a challenge this presents to a world which takes pleasure in continually increasing human needs and so makes itself more and more dependent on the material world.

I have not been able to reach this extreme degree of detachment. I have my little hut, which is simple enough, just one small room with a thatched roof, but it is solidly built of brick with a concrete floor. I have also a table, a chair and a bed, which are luxuries for a *sannyasi*, but I have not been able to learn to sit and sleep always on the floor. I have also my books and my typewriter, but these are not really 'mine', any more than the hut and the furniture – they are, as we say, 'allowed for my use'. A *sannyasi* is one who does not *possess* anything, not even the clothes on his back. He has renounced all 'property'. This is the real renunciation which is demanded, the renunciation of 'I' and 'mine'. A *sannyasi* is one who is totally detached from the world and from himself. It is detachment which is the key-word. It does not matter so much what material possessions you have, so long as you are not attached to them. You must be ready to give up everything, not only material attachments but also human attachments – father, mother, wife, children – everything that you have. But the one thing which you have to abandon unconditionally is your 'self'. If you can give up your self, your 'ego', you can have anything you like, wife and family, houses and lands – but who is able to give up his self?

Poverty – the poverty of spirit of the Sermon on the Mount – is a total detachment from the material world. It is to recognize that everything comes from God – our bodies, our breath, our very existence. We cannot properly possess anything – not even our own bodies, as St Benedict says.[2] We can only receive everything from God at every moment – our life, our food, our clothing, our shelter, our books, our friends. Everything comes from God, created anew at every moment. If there were not this constantly renewed creation, everything would sink into nothingness. People speak of Buddhism and Hinduism as world-renouncing religions, and then they are surprised to find that these world-renouncers built temples of fantastic beauty and covered the walls of the caves, which they hollowed out, with paintings of infinite refinement. But this is precisely because they were detached from the world. When you are detached from the world, you see everything coming from the hands of God, always fresh and beautiful. Everything is a symbol of God. The modern age has banished God from the world and therefore it has also banished beauty. Everything has become 'profane', exiled from the sphere of the 'holy', and therefore everything has lost its meaning. For the holy is the source of truth no less than of beauty. It relates the world to the one, transcendent Reality from which the world derives its existence, its meaning and its loveliness.

This kind of detachment from the world is in no way opposed to service of the world or 'commitment' to the world. It is freedom from all *selfish* attachment. It is only when you are free from self – that is, free from self-love and self-will – that you can really serve the world. You can then see things as they are and use them as they should be used. The poet or artist has to be detached from the world if he is to reflect it truly in his art. The scientist must be detached from things if he is to deal with them scientifically. But the saint needs a more radical detachment than either. He must be detached from his very self. He does not belong to himself but to God. This includes not only the conscious self but also the unconscious. He must break all those bonds of attachment which are rooted in the unconscious, which have grown up from childhood and become a second nature. This is the work of a life-time, and for most people it will not end in this life. Purgatory is the breaking of the bonds of attachment which remain in us at death.

What, then, is chastity? It is detachment from the flesh, just as poverty is detachment from the world. Of course, this does not mean that the flesh is evil, any more than the world is evil. The world and the flesh were created by God and are destined for the resurrection. They become the source of evil when we are attached to them – that is, when we put them in the place of God. We have to sacrifice the world and the flesh, that is, to make them holy (*sacrum facere*) by offering them to God. 'I appeal to you therefore, brethren, by the mercies of God, to present your bodies as a living sacrifice, holy and acceptable to God.'[3] 'The body is not meant for immorality, but for the Lord.'[4] This is the essential condition of chastity. It doesn't matter whether you are married or unmarried; in either case the body has to be offered to the Lord – that is, we have to be radically detached from our passions and desires and surrender them to God. Then they become holy. The married man is joined to the Lord through his wife, the wife through her husband. The unmarried man or woman is joined to the Lord without intermediary: the marriage takes place within. Every man and woman is both male and female, and the male and the female have to be married within. In heaven, when 'the male shall be as the female, and that which is without as that which is within', as one of the 'Sayings of Jesus' says, there will be neither marrying nor giving in marriage. Then our human nature will be complete, the male and the female having achieved their essential unity in the body of Christ.

How, then, to understand obedience? Poverty is detachment from the world, chastity is detachment from the flesh, obedience is detachment from the self. This is the most radical detachment of all. But what is the self? The self is the principle of reason and responsibility in us, it is the root of freedom, it is what makes us men. But this self is not autonomous; it is subject to a law – to what in India is called *dharma*, which St Thomas Aquinas called the universal Reason, the Law of the universe. The great illusion is to consider that the self has an absolute freedom, that it is a law to itself. This is the original sin. In fact, the self can never act independently. It must either act in dependence on *dharma*, that is the law of reason, or it will become subject to another law, the law of nature, of passion and desire, that is, the powers of the unconscious.

This is the drama of paradise. Man was placed in the garden of this world and given to eat of all the trees, of the senses, the feelings, the appetites, the desires – all were open to him. But the tree of knowledge of good and evil – the conscience by which we know what is right and wrong – was not left within his power. For that he is dependent on a higher power, and the moment he eats of it and seeks to make himself the master of his destiny, he loses his autonomy and becomes the slave of the powers of nature – the other gods, who take the place of the one God. The self must either be dependent on God, the universal Law, and acquire true freedom, or else it loses its freedom in subjection to nature, to the unconscious. This is the essential nature of the self; it is not a static entity, complete in itself. It is a power of self-transcendence. It is the power to give one's self totally to another, to transcend one's self by surrendering to the higher Self, the Atman, the Spirit within. When this is done, we live from the principle of Life within, from the universal Law of Reason, we are 'established in Brahman'.[5] This is wisdom and joy and immortality. This is what man was created for – this is true obedience.

TWO

The Sacred Mystery

The whole question is, what is the true Self? What is the true Centre of man's being? Is it the ego, making itself independent, seeking to be master of the world, or is there an 'I' beyond this, a deeper Centre of personal being, which is grounded in the Truth, which is one with the universal Self, the Law of the universe? This is the great discovery of Indian thought, the discovery of the Self, the Atman, the Ground of personal being, which is one with the Brahman, the Ground of universal being. It is not reached by thought; on the contrary, it is only reached by transcending thought. Reason, like the self of which it is the faculty, has to transcend itself. As long as it remains turned towards the senses, to the material world, it will always remain defective, unable to discover the Truth. But the moment it turns inwards to its Source[1] and knows itself in its Ground by a pure intuition, then it knows the truth of its own being and the being of the world, and then it becomes really free. 'You will know the truth, and the truth will make you free.'[2] This is redemption, to be set free from the senses and the material world and to discover their Ground and Source in the Self, which is the Word of God within. The Fall of Man is the fall from this Ground, this Centre of freedom and immortality, into subjection to the senses and this material world, and Reason is the serpent. Reason can either be subject to the eternal Law, the universal Reason, and then it becomes Wisdom, it knows the Self, or it can seek to be the master of the world, and then it becomes demonic. It is the demon of the modern world. In every generation the Fall of Man is repeated, but never, perhaps, on a wider scale than today.

How then to recover from the Fall, how to return to the Centre? This is the problem of the modern world, but it has been the problem of the world from the beginning. Every ancient culture, as Mircea Eliade has shown,[3] built its life round such a Centre. It might be a building, a temple, a city, or simply the home; it might be a place – a mountain, a grove, a burial ground; or it might be a person – a priest or king or seer. But always it was a point where contact could be made with the Source of being. It was a point where heaven and earth converge, where human life is open to the infinite Transcendence. This was the essential thing, to keep contact with the Transcendent, so that human life did not become closed on itself. But the modern world has removed every such point of contact. Everything has become profane, that is, outside the sphere of the holy. Temple and palace, priest and king, sacred grove and mountain, all must be abolished, so that the world of nature and the world of man alike may be emptied of a transcendent significance, of any ultimate meaning. No wonder that there is a rebellion among the young against this drab, one-dimensional world. Young people now come to India from the West, seeking to recover the sense of the sacred, the inner meaning of life, which has been lost in the West. But India too is losing it rapidly. Wherever modern civilization spreads, all holiness, all sense of the sacred, all awareness of a transcendent Reality disappears. This is just another Fall of Man.

But, thank God, there are still sacred places in India – sacred mountains and caves, sacred rivers and trees and plants and animals, sacred places where people go on pilgrimage. There are still temples where the old, sacred rites continue, and holy men to whom people go to find God. Always there is a sense of a transcendent Mystery, of an ultimate Reality behind the appearances. An Indian village, with all its poverty and squalor and disease, has still a sacred character, of which a modern suburb with all its affluence and cleanliness and health services has not a trace. For an Indian villager, however poor and despised he may be, birth and marriage and death are still sacred mysteries. Through the traditional rituals which surround them, he is brought into relation with the ultimate Mystery. The festivals of the gods throughout the year keep him in touch with a transcendent world beyond the miseries of this present life. Is this the 'opium of the people'? If so, it is an opium which opens the eyes to reality, as many young people today have found. Opium, or any other hallucinatory drug, opens up the world of the unconscious, the world of the gods and demons, in which man lived before the scientific age – a dangerous world, which can lead to madness but can also lead to God.

Modern science and technology are the fruit of the tree of the knowledge of good and evil. They are not evil in themselves, but they become evil when, as usually happens, they are separated from wisdom. Science is the lowest form of human knowledge – the knowledge of the material world through the discursive reason. Philosophy is above science, because it goes beyond the material world and explores the world of thought, but it is still confined to discursive reason. Theology is above philosophy, because it is open to the world of transcendent reality, but its methods are still those of science and philosophy. It is only wisdom which can transcend reason and know the Truth, not discursively but intuitively, not by its reflection in the world of the senses but in its Ground, where knowing is also being. The knowledge of science when separated from wisdom is always a knowledge of good and evil. Every advance in science brings a corresponding evil in its train. The knowledge of medicine, which has radically changed the prospects of life, brings with it the disaster of over-population. The knowledge of physics and chemistry, which creates technology and brings the amenities of life, creates also the atom bomb and brings pollution of the earth, the sea and the sky. All this is due to the fact that science and technology have developed without relation to heaven – to the transcendent Reality, the universal Law, the Tao, which keeps heaven and earth in harmony. If mankind is to survive – and it is his survival which is now threatened – it can only be through a total change of heart, a *metanoia*, which will make science subordinate to wisdom. The discursive reason which seeks to dominate the world and imprisons man in the narrow world of the conscious mind must be dethroned, and must acknowledge its dependence on the transcendent Mystery, which is beyond the rational consciousness.

What is this 'transcendent Mystery', this 'ultimate Truth', this 'universal Law'? These are words we use to express the inexpressible. This is the whole problem of life, which continually baffles our reason. The ultimate meaning and purpose of life cannot be expressed, cannot properly be thought. It is present everywhere, in everything, yet it always escapes our grasp. It is the 'Ground' of all existence, that from which all things come, to which all things return, but which never appears. It is 'within' all things, 'above' all things, 'beyond' all things, but it cannot be identified with anything. Without it nothing could exist, without it nothing can be known, yet it is itself unknown. It is that by which everything is known, yet which itself remains unknown. It is 'unseen but seeing, unheard but hearing, unperceived but perceiving, unknown but knowing'.[4] This is the mystery upon which both Indian and Chinese thought lighted in the sixth century before Christ. They called it Brahman, Atman, Nirvana, Tao, but these are only names for what cannot be named. We speak of 'God', but this also is only a name for this inexpressible Mystery.

This Mystery lies behind all religion, from the most primitive to the most advanced. Thus it is said of the American Indians: 'The Tlingit do not divide the universe arbitrarily into so many different quarters ruled by so many supernatural beings. On the contrary, supernatural power impresses them as a vast immensity, one in kind and impersonal, inscrutable as to its nature, but whenever manifesting itself to men, taking a personal, and it might be said, a human personal form in whatever aspect it displays itself. Thus the sky spirit is the ocean of supernatural energy as it manifests itself in the sky, the sea spirit as it manifests itself in the sea, the bear spirit as it manifests itself in the bear, the rock spirit as it manifests itself in the rock . . . For this reason there is but one name for this supernatural power, Yok, a name which is affixed to any specific manifestation of it.'[5]

In the same way, 'the religious faith of the Dakota is not in his gods as such. It is in a mysterious and intangible something of which they are only the embodiment . . . Each one will worship some of these divinities and neglect and despise others; but the great object of all their worship, whatever its chosen medium, is the

Taku Wakan, which is the supernatural and mysterious.
No one term can express the full meaning of the Dakota's
Wakan. It comprehends all mystery, secret power and
divinity.'[6] This, which is true of the American Indians
and seems to be the basic pattern of all primitive religion, is also true of Hinduism. All the gods (and
goddesses) are but manifestations of the one, infinite,
eternal Brahman. Behind all the fantastic figures of
Hindu mythology, behind the vast forest of images in a
Hindu temple, there is the presence of the One 'without
a second', the unutterable mystery of the Brahman.

Perhaps the most radical insight into this mystery was
that of the Buddha. He was the first to tear away the veil
of appearances and face the stark reality which lay
behind. 'All is sorrow, all is passing, all is unreal.'[7] This
is the most radical insight into our human condition.
Until one has realized this, one has not learned to face
reality. This world in itself has no reality at all. It is in
perpetual flux, as Heraclitus said, without meaning or
consistency. It is *maya* in the strictest sense, a pure
illusion, like a mirage, a conjuror's show, like the form
of a snake superimposed on a rope. It is absolutely
empty. This is the horror of darkness, of emptiness, of
nothingness, which lurks under all the outward appearances of life. To cling to the appearances is to court unending sorrow, it is to live perpetually under an illusion.
The existentialist today has realized something of this
insight of the Buddha. He has seen into the nothingness,
the absurdity, the meaninglessness of life. It needed a
doctrine of materialism, which mistakes the flux of
matter for reality, to recover this sense of the 'vanity' of
life, which the Preacher discovered long ago – 'Vanity of
vanities! All is vanity.'[8] This is a deeply Buddhist
thought.

But having seen through the appearances, having removed the veil, the Buddha discovered the Reality. 'There is, brethren, an unborn, a not become, a not made, a not compounded. If there were not, brethren, this that is unborn, not become, not made, not compounded, there could not be any escape from what is born, become, made, compounded.'[9] This is the insight which brings deliverance – to see through this world which everyone takes to be real and to discover Reality. And yet that Reality cannot be described except in negative terms. The Buddha called it Nirvana, but that also is a negative term and the Buddha steadfastly refused to define it. It is a 'blowing out' of the flame of life, a passing over to the other shore; it is a condition where no 'craving' remains, where *nothing* remains. It is the annihilation of this world 'where there is no this world, and no other world'.[10]

How difficult it is to face that absolute nothingness, that total emptiness. This is what death puts before us – utter annihilation, and to fall into this is surely what is meant by hell. It is to lose all touch with reality, to succumb to the final illusion, to lose one's soul. But if death is faced, as the Buddha faced it, then the illusion is seen through, the nothingness is found to be the ultimate Reality, the emptiness is found to be absolute Fullness, just as at the moment when Christ cried out on the cross, 'My God, my God, why hast thou forsaken me?' and surrendered himself to death, the kingdom of God came, the world was transformed. 'Truly, I say to you, today you will be with me in paradise.'[11]

This is the mystery. On the one side death, destruction, nothingness, the negation of being, which is *maya*, the great illusion. But on the other side, where the illusion is seen through, then death itself is found to be eternal life;

Siva, the 'destroyer' of the world, is he who re-creates it; the nothingness and the void of Nirvana is the ultimate Truth; the ultimate Reality is not-being rather than being. Did not the great Benedictine monk, Augustine Baker, describe the soul's union with God as 'the union of the nothing with the Nothing'? For God and the soul are surely not 'things'; to lose one's soul is to save it and even God must die before he can be known for what he is.

This is the deep truth behind the *advaita* doctrine of Sankara.[12] When considered apart from Brahman – the absolute Reality – this world has no reality at all. It is pure illusion, absolute nothingness. It has no more reality than a conjuror's show, or the form of a snake which is imagined when a rope is seen in the dark. Wisdom consists in the awakening to the unreality of this world, to the knowledge that 'all is Brahman'. But once this is realized, then the world recovers all its reality. Apart from Brahman, it is nothing at all, but when it is known as Brahman, then it is Reality itself, it is the absolute Fullness of being. Everything that exists in this world, down to the minutest particle of matter, exists eternally in Brahman. Here we see everything separated in space and time, changing from one moment to the next, but there everything is present to everything else in an absolute simplicity of being 'without duality'. Here all is multiplicity and change, there everything is one in eternal repose. Yet we must not think that the dynamism has gone out of the world, that all is dead and lifeless. There is nothing here, no positive value whatso-ever, no being, energy, life, intelligence, virtue, grace, no particular beauty of earth or sky or sea, which is not there present in its totality. It is only to our consciousness limited by the senses that things appear separate and divided, changing and passing away; when we transcend this consciousness and get beyond both sense and reason, then we shall see things as they are, as God sees them. For God sees the whole creation, in all its expanse in space and time, in the simple vision of his own infinite and eternal being. For him the world does not come into being and pass away: it is present to him in a timeless 'now' and at a spaceless point. Aquinas and Sankara are here agreed. In God, the absolute Being, there is no division, or 'composition' of any kind. He is 'without duality' and sees and knows all things in himself as they exist eternally in identity with him. Everything – and every person – exists eternally in God as God.[13] This is the truth of *advaita*, a truth as Catholic as it is Hindu.

If there is ever to be a meeting of the religious traditions of the world, it can only be on this basis. It cannot be based on belief in 'God' because neither the Buddhist nor the Jain believe in 'God'. 'God' is a name for that ultimate Mystery when it is seen in relation to man, as Creator, Lord, Saviour, or whatever it may be. Of this 'God' it is reasonable to ask whether he exists or not. But of the Godhead, of the ultimate Truth, one cannot ask whether it exists. It is the Ground of all existence. To exist is to 'stand out' (*ex-sistere*) from this Ground, but the Ground itself does not 'exist'. It is that by which all things, including God the Creator, exist. This is the great Tao, of which it is said, 'The Tao which can be uttered is not the eternal Tao, the name that can be named is not the eternal name. Without a name it is the origin of heaven and earth, with a name it is the mother of all things.'[14] It is the '*nirguna* Brahman', the Brahman 'without attributes' and without relation to anything, as distinguished from '*saguna* Brahman', Brahman 'with attributes', who is the Creator, the Lord (Isvara). It is the 'Dharmakaya' of the Buddha, the 'body of Reality', the ultimate Being, of which the Buddha himself is a manifestation. It is the One of Plotinus which is beyond the Mind (the Nous) and can only be known in ecstasy. In Christian terms it is the abyss of the Godhead, the 'divine darkness' of Dionysius, which 'exceeds all existence'[15] and cannot be named, of which the Persons of the Godhead are the manifestations.

But if this Mystery cannot be expressed or described, cannot even be said to exist, how is it to be known? Well, of course, it cannot properly be known. It is not among things that are known. It is the Knower. Behind all knowledge is the Knower, which can never appear, never be seen, never become an object. 'How should one know the Knower?'[16] It is the subject, not the object, of thought, the 'I' that thinks, not the 'I' that is thought. It is the Ground of consciousness just as it is the Ground of existence. It is that from which all thought springs but which cannot be thought. Yet there is a point beyond thought, where this becomes known, not as an object of thought, nor even as a subject as distinct from an object, but in an identity of subject and object, of being and knowing. This is the experience of the Self, the Atman, beyond being in so far as being is an object of thought, beyond thought in so far as thought is a reflection, a concept of being. It is pure awareness of being, pure delight in being – *saccidananda*, being, knowledge, bliss. It is Nirvana, the ultimate State, the supreme Wisdom, beyond which it is impossible to go. 'O Wisdom, gone, gone, gone beyond, gone to the other shore.'[17]

THREE

The Revelation of the Mystery

So all existence, all thought, loses itself in a void, a darkness, an abyss, where all landmarks fail. No wonder people are afraid of going beyond being, beyond thought – one may lose one's self entirely. And yet – 'he who will lose his life [or "soul"] shall save it.' If we do not make this plunge, we shall never reach the Truth. Every great religious tradition has known this, not only Buddhist or Hindu, but Jewish, Muslim and Christian. Without this basis in the Transcendent, the Inexpressible, all revelations would lose their meaning. They would become idols. Nothing can be spoken about God which does not become false if it is not referred to this transcendent Mystery. To say that God is good or wise or just, or even that he is Being, Truth or the Absolute, is simply untrue, if these words are used in their ordinary sense. They are signs which point beyond themselves to the Inexpressible. This is true of the Christian God no less than of any other. He – or It – remains the unfathomable Mystery. The incarnation – the words, the actions, the 'history' of Christ – is an expression in human terms of this Mystery, but the Mystery remains. The incarnation belongs to the world of signs – it makes the reality present, but it cannot disclose it. The whole world is a sign of this Mystery, 'from Brahma to a blade of grass'. It is everywhere and nowhere. Everything speaks of it – the evil as well as the good, the pain and misery of life as well as the joy and the beauty – but it remains hidden.

To speak of it is already to betray it: it is known in the silence of the world and of the self.

And yet we must speak of it – it is itself the source of speech. It is the Word – the Word uttered in the darkness, the Word that is spoken in the silence of the Father.[1] When this Word is spoken, then the abyss of the Godhead reveals itself as Father, as the Ground, the Source, the Origin. Of this it has been said: 'There was something undefined and complete, coming into existence before heaven and earth. How still it was and formless, standing alone, and undergoing no change, reaching everywhere and in no danger of being exhausted. It may be regarded as the Mother of all things.'[2] Christian tradition has always spoken of it as the Father, because Jesus himself knew it as Abba, Father, but it can also be called the Mother. The Hindu knows it as both Father and Mother, and the name of the great god Siva can be masculine, feminine or neuter. We need to know it as both Mother and Father. It is the womb from which the Son is born. As Krishna in the Gita says: 'Great Brahman is the womb in which I place the seed, whence comes the birth of all beings.'[3] The Word is the seed in which all creation is contained. The whole creation comes forth eternally in the Word from the abyss of Being which is both Father and Mother. Before anything comes into being in time, it exists eternally in the Word, or rather, since there is no before or after, let us say that beyond its appearance in space and time, everything has an eternal existence in the Word. To discern this eternal Ground of every event in space and time is wisdom.

The Father utters himself eternally in his Word, and in that Word everything is contained, every particle of matter, every movement of life, every human soul. That

is our eternal being, our being in the Word; to realize
this is eternal life. The Fall is our fall from this state of
being, from the being, knowledge and bliss of our
eternal existence in the Word. The Fall is our fall into
this present mode of consciousness, where everything is
divided, centred on itself and set in conflict with others.
The Fall is the fall into self-consciousness, that is, into a
consciousness centred in the self which has lost touch with
the eternal Ground of consciousness, which is the true
Self. It is not that self-consciousness, as such, is evil. Man
was intended to grow from an identification with nature –
the unconsciousness of the womb – to the consciousness
of the Self. But this Self is found in God. It comes forth
from the divine darkness in the Word, as an eternal
expression of his being. The Godhead contains within
its infinite being innumerable possibilities of finite being,
and each of us is an eternal expression of one of these
possibilities of being. Each of us is a word within the
one Word. To realize one's self is to realize one's eternal
'idea' in the Word. Sin is the failure to realize the
Self. It is to fall into a separate, divided self, a self
which is essentially illusory, since it has lost touch with
its real being in God. In this sense all this world –
the world of our present mode of consciousness – is
maya.

The real world is the world as it exists eternally in God.
What we see is the shadow of this real world. Our
senses present everything to us divided in space and
time; our reason, which is based on the senses, can never
get beyond these limitations. Science is essentially an
illusory knowledge, a knowledge of the appearance of
things in space and time. It is a knowledge of the real,
but of the real as it appears in space and time. It is like
the knowledge which our senses give us of the sun and the

moon and the stars in the sky. There is a real sun and moon and stars, but the way in which they appear to us is illusory. The utmost elaboration of physics and astronomy does not dispel this illusion. To see the world as it is, the sun, the moon, the stars, the earth and everything in it, would be to see it in the Word, where every movement in space and time is gathered to a point. It is like listening to a symphony, where you have to follow note by note and to distinguish every instrument and to wait for three-quarters of an hour until it is completed. But an integral vision would grasp the symphony as a whole, in every detail of its parts, in indivisible unity. We begin to experience this ourselves as we grow familiar with a symphony, a poem, a painting – we grasp the whole, in all its parts, and the parts in the whole. If we could grasp our whole life like this, know everything that has moulded our being in its integral wholeness, then we should begin to know ourselves. This is what is promised us in the beatific vision – to know ourselves and everyone and everything in their integral and indivisible unity in the Word.

We must not think that anything is lost in this vision of the whole. When we know things in general, we lose sight of the particulars, and when we know the particulars, we lose sight of the general, but here it is not so. It is more like those rare moments of vision when everything seems to focus on a particular point, it may be a loved person, a poem, a sunset, a moment of pain or ecstasy. Then the barriers of space and time begin to fall – everything comes together in unity; this is a foretaste of that unending bliss. This is the natural state of our being; we were born for this vision of eternity. We have fallen into our present state of consciousness in space and time. This is the meaning of sin; it is a divided consciousness. Redemption – at-one-ment – is the return to unity. This is also the resurrection, the awakening to our true being in the Word. Christ at the resurrection returned to himself, to his eternal being in the Word of God. He manifested on earth that state of undivided being in the Word beyond the limitations of space and time. He could appear and disappear because he was no longer bound by space and time. He awoke from the sleep of death to the eternal reality. He did not go to some other world; he became wholly present to this world. There is no 'other' world to which he could go – at least, there may be other worlds in space and time, but it was not to one of these that he went. He passed beyond space and time, beyond the limits of our present mode of existence, of our present mode of consciousness. In so doing he 'realized' this world in its totality, in its being in the Word. He 'realized' himself, and in himself all humanity, in his and its eternal being. In his surrender to death on the cross all the pain and agony of mankind was concentrated at a single point, and passed through death to immortality. There is no pain of any creature from the beginning to the end of time which was not 'known' at this point and thus transmuted. To know all things in the Word is thus to know all the suffering of the world transfigured by the resurrection, somehow reconciled and atoned in eternal life.

What is one to say about reincarnation? Sankara said that 'the Lord is the only transmigrator'. This makes it meaningful. There is one Self who becomes incarnate in humanity. He is the indweller in the heart of every human being. It is this Self, the indwelling Spirit, who passes from life to life. 'As a man lays aside outworn garments and takes others that are new, so the body-dweller puts away outworn bodies and goes to others that are new.'[4] Mankind as a whole, humanity in the total course of its history, is the body of this one Spirit. All men, as Aquinas says, are one Man.[5] It is this one Man who fell in Adam and who is redeemed in Christ. Christ is the Self of redeemed humanity. Every man by his birth into humanity inherits the sin of the one Man, and has a separate, divided, fallen self. But Christ on the cross redeemed this fallen Man; he took upon himself the sin – the *karma* – of fallen humanity and set it free. He assumed the body of fallen humanity and made it the body of God. Christ is now the Self of redeemed mankind restoring it to its being in the Word. Christ is therefore incarnate in every man, or rather he is incarnate in the whole universe. For as all men are one Man and form the body of Christ, so the whole universe is one body, one organic whole, which comes to a head in man. The evolution of matter from the beginning leads to the evolution of consciousness in man; it is the universe itself which becomes conscious in man. It was the whole of this organic process of evolution from matter to life and consciousness in man that Christ assumed into himself. It was God's 'purpose which he set forth in Christ as a plan for the fullness of time, to unite all things in him, things in heaven and things on earth'.[6] We can say therefore with Ramanuja that 'the whole universe of animate and inanimate beings is the body of the supreme Person who rules it from within',[7] not that the universe modifies the being of God in any way, but that, being assumed into the divine life through the incarnation, it becomes the body of Christ. Christ is the indwelling Spirit, the Self, of the universe, who redeems it from the dispersion in space and time, and unites all its diverse tendencies in one body in himself. Or to put it in evolutionary terms, he is the term of the evolution of the universe, which evolving in space and time achieves its true being in him. Matter is unified in human consciousness, and human consciousness is unified in the divine. This, then, is the full meaning of the incarnation, the assumption of the whole universe and the whole of humanity into the divine life. It was this which was revealed in the resurrection.

The body of Christ was formed from the matter of the universe, from the actual particles, protons, electrons, neutrons, atoms, molecules, which constitute matter. Just as these particles are organized into living cells and begin to perform the functions of life; and just as the living cells are formed into animal organisms and begin to perform the functions of animal life; and as the animal organism with its atoms and molecules and cells is formed into a human being and begins to exercise rational activity; so in the resurrection these same particles of matter, these living cells, this animal organism, were formed into a 'spiritual body', a body filled with divine life and participating in the divine consciousness. 'In him the whole fullness of deity dwells bodily.'[8] The evolution of the universe is from matter to life, to consciousness in man, and from human consciousness to divine life and consciousness. The resurrection was the point of emergence of this divine life in man, but the divine life had been present from the beginning. The Spirit, the Self, is latent in matter from the beginning. 'The Spirit of God was moving over the face of the waters.'[9] It is the inner movement of the Spirit, immanent in nature, which brings about the evolution of matter and life into consciousness, and the same Spirit at work in human consciousness, latent in every man, is always at work leading to divine life. At the resurrection this divine life was manifested, the Spirit took possession of a human body, and the universe through that human body emerged into divine consciousness. 'The first man Adam became a living being; the last Adam became a life-giving spirit.'[10]

FOUR

Who Am I?

I look at the flowers which are growing in the garden outside my window – golden-orange marigolds and crimson Christmas roses. They come up out of the darkness of the earth, which is itself the shadow of the divine darkness, the abyss of being from which everything comes. They come out of this darkness into the light of the Word, radiant with its brightness, reflecting its glory. The impulse which quickens them in the earth and makes them thrust into the light is the movement of the Spirit, the divine Sakti,[1] immanent in the earth. They come up into my consciousness, as the light touches the nerves of my eye and an image is formed in my mind. It is the same light of the Word which shines in them and in my consciousness. I see them in the light of the Word. And the same Spirit which stirs in them stirs in me, awakening feelings of joy and delight in their beauty. They are in me and I am in them, and both of us are in the Word and in the Spirit. This is a theophany. The Father speaks his Word and these flowers spring into being. He speaks again and my consciousness awakens to delight in their beauty. He sends forth his Spirit and they are created.[2] The same Spirit moves the flowers to spring and me to contemplate them: both in them and in me it is the one Lord who rejoices in his works.

Who am I? Let me try to answer this question. I am this person who sits here thinking and meditating. I am aware of myself sitting and thinking and meditating. I am aware of my body which occupies the space of my cell, which looks out on the flowers in the garden and hears the birds singing, and at the same time I am aware of my mind, which reflects on my body and the world around me, which names these sights and sounds and expresses my thoughts in these words. But I am much more than this. I have a long history now of sixty-five years, in which my body and my mind have undergone innumerable changes. My body was originally formed from an ovum and a sperm in my mother's body, and this ovum and sperm were formed of matter which came into the bloodstream of my father and mother from the world outside. I am formed of the matter of the universe and am linked through it to the remotest stars in time and space. My body has passed through all the stages of evolution through which matter has passed over millions of years. I have been present when matter was first formed into atoms and molecules, when the living cell appeared. I have passed through every stage from protoplasm to fish and animal and man. If I could know myself, I would know matter and life, animal and man, since all are contained within me. In all this long evolution my mind has been developing with my body. There was a mind latent in matter, latent in the living cell, which has gradually emerged into consciousness. My mind has recapitulated every stage of human consciousness from the most primitive state of awareness to the reflective consciousness I enjoy now. But most of this remains buried in my unconscious. How little of myself do I really know. My conscious knowledge is only the tip of an iceberg which reaches down to the depths of the abyss from which my existence first emerged.

How can I get to know myself? Not by thinking, for thinking only reflects my conscious being, but by meditating. Meditation goes beyond the conscious mind

into the unconscious. In meditation I can become aware
of the ground of my being in matter, in life, in human
consciousness. I can experience my solidarity with the
universe, with the remotest star in outer space and with
the minutest particle in the atom. I can experience my
solidarity with every living thing, with the earth, with
these flowers and coconut trees, with the birds and
squirrels, with every human being. I can get beyond all
these outer forms of things in time and space and discover the Ground from which they all spring. I can know
the Father, the Origin, the Source, beyond being and
not-being, the One 'without a second'. I can know the
birth of all things from this Ground, their coming into
being in the Word. They come into being not in time and
space, but eternally, beyond time, in the Word. The
Word is the self-manifestation of the Father and the Self
of all beings. I have existed eternally in this Word and so
have all these things, this earth, these flowers and birds
and squirrels. We came forth in the Word from the
Father beyond time and space, and there we stand
eternally before him.

But who, then, am I? It is not my body which is my
self, my body which has undergone so many trans-
migrations in space and time. It is not my mind which
thinks which is my self, for my thoughts only know the
surface of life and I cannot know myself by thought. But
in meditation I pass beyond my body which exists in
space and time and beyond my thoughts which reflect
my body-consciousness. I discover my ground in the
Word, my real Self which exists eternally in God and
with God. Am I then God? No, I am a thought of God,
a word of God. In his one Word, God expresses an
infinite multiplicity of thoughts; every created being is a
thought of God, a word of God to which he gives ex-

pression. 'He spoke, and it came to be; he commanded, and it stood forth.'[3] All the myriad stars in the sky, the galaxies receding into outer space, are thoughts and words of God, gathered into unity in the one consciousness of the Word. But within this one consciousness there is an infinite multiplicity of centres of consciousness. Every human being is such a centre of consciousness in which the one consciousness is broken up and, as it were, divided. Through our consciousness, functioning through a material body, the one eternal and infinite Being is reflected in time and space. The world we see through our senses and reflect in our consciousness, is the one eternal Reality reflected in space and time. This world is not unreal; it is the real world, but reflected as in a mirror. To mistake the reflection for the reality, to think that the world as it appears to the senses is real in itself, is illusion. As Sankara says: 'The whole multiplicity of creatures, existing under name and form, in so far as it has the supreme Being for its essence, is true; if regarded as self-dependent, is untrue.'[4]

I look out on this world of things around me, each one separated in space, each one moving in time, and beyond this comparatively stable world I know that there is an almost infinite dispersion of matter in space, a perpetual flux of movement in time. The one Word has gone out of itself, has reflected itself in this ocean of matter, the one Spirit is at work with its infinite energy, building up this matter in time. In my consciousness this diffusion of matter, this flux of becoming, begins to be ordered in space and time. But there is a window in my consciousness where I can look out on eternity, or rather where this eternal Reality looks out on the world of space and time through me. When I turn back beyond my senses and beyond my reason and pass through this door into eternal life, then I discover my true Self, then I begin to see the world as it really is. This is the archetypal world, not known in its diffusion in space and time, not reflected through a human consciousness dependent on a material body, but the world in its eternal reality, gathered into the one consciousness of the Word. Here all is one, united in a simple vision of being. All the long evolution of matter and life and man, all my own history from the first moment that I became a living cell, all the stages of my consciousness and that of all human beings, is here recapitulated, brought to a point, and I know myself as the Self of all, the one Word eternally spoken in time.

But does this mean that here all differences and distinctions disappear? Does this mean that I am God? Here I must remember that what I am trying to describe is a mystical reality, which cannot properly be expressed in human terms. I am straining human speech in order to try to bring it within the grasp of my mind. If I am using the ordinary language of rational thought, then certainly I am not God, and to say that this world is God is as false as to say that it exists of itself. If I try to find words to express that transcendent Reality, I have to use images and metaphors, which help to turn my mind towards the truth, and allow Truth itself to enlighten it. I can say that that eternal world is like the white light of the sun, in which all the colours of the rainbow are present and in which each retains its own distinctive character. Or I can say that it is like a symphony in which all the notes are heard in a single perfect harmony, but in which each has its own particular time and place. Or I can say that it is like a multitude of thoughts gathered together in a single mind which comprehends them in a single idea embracing all. Or going deeper, I can say that it is like a communion of persons in love, in which each understands the other and is one with the other. 'I in them and thou in me, that they may become perfectly one.'[5] This is as far as human words can go. All are one in the Word and the Word is one with the Father.

FIVE

The One and the Many

'Of this I am certain,' wrote Walter de la Mare, 'that it will be impossible for me to free myself, to escape from this world, unless in peace and amity I can take every shred of it, every friend and every enemy, all that these eyes have seen, these senses discovered. This I *know*.' Or as Rilke said: 'We are the bees of the invisible . . . This earth has no other refuge except to become invisible in us, who through one part of our nature have a share in the invisible and can increase our holding in invisibility during our being here. Only in us can this intimate and enduring transformation of the visible into an invisible, no longer dependent on visibility and tangibility, be accomplished, since our destiny is continually growing at once more actual and invisible within us.'[1]

Every poet has caught a glimpse of this eternal Reality and seen the world transfigured by it, but his vision is usually only for a moment or for a limited time. He himself has not been transfigured. But we seek this total transfiguration. The whole creation has to pass into human consciousness, to become invisible in man, and man himself – we ourselves – have to pass into our Self, to transcend ourselves, and become one with that eternal Truth.

But the point is that nothing is lost in the process, the world becomes more, not less, real when it is realized in the divine consciousness. The world which is seen by a poet – a Dante, a Chaucer, a Shakespeare – is more, not less, real than the world which is seen by the ordinary man. Matter diffused in space without consciousness is at the furthest point of unreality. When it is organized into a living cell, it begins to acquire more reality. But it is only when it enters into consciousness in man that its reality begins to appear. But even so, in ordinary human consciousness the world is only partially real. The world of science is a world of abstractions, of certain aspects of reality, which can be measured in space and time, abstracted from the whole. The poet is nearer to a vision of the whole, the world begins to be transfigured in him, but it is only the mystic who is present at the final transfiguration, who catches a glimpse of the world transfigured in the divine light. Yet this is promised to us all in the resurrection. 'We shall be changed. For this perishable nature must put on the imperishable, and this mortal nature must put on immortality.'[2] The human consciousness will be transfigured by the divine light, no longer conditioned by time and space, and matter will be transfigured in us. We shall see the whole creation in its eternal Truth, when we ourselves have been so changed, when we have become one with that eternal Truth, that Word in whom all things subsist, and who is one with the Father, the ultimate Ground of reality.

Everything will be present there in its total reality, not in general but in particular, each of us totally present to himself in his integral being, body and soul. Moreover, all time will be there. Eternity is not a timeless state in the sense that events that take place in time will simply have ceased to be, but rather in the sense that time is fulfilled, that the events have reached their consummation. The whole of the past will be present to me, not in its dispersion in time, in its state of becoming, but in its fullness, its complete being. Eternity is 'tota et simul' – the total and simultaneous enjoyment of unending life.[3]

Everyone and everything will be totally and simul-
taneously present to everyone and everything. All the
multiplicity of creation will be there, but it will be there
in its unity. When we think of unity, we lose sight of the
multiplicity; when we think of multiplicity, we lose
sight of the unity. But in eternity the many are contained
in the One without losing their individuality. Each
human being is a focus of the divine Light which shines
through all equally, but each receives it according to its
capacity. Each is conscious only of the divine Light itself
and loses itself in its radiance; each is filled to capacity
and knows no difference, yet the distinctions and the
differences remain. The experience is of 'non-duality',
of immersion in the divine Being, Knowledge and Bliss,
yet no two souls are the same and the experience of each
is unique. This was the very purpose of creation – that
each unique, individual being should participate in its
own way in the divine Being, should realize its eternal
'idea' in God, should 'become' God by participation,
God expressing himself through that unique being.

Creation loses any meaning if there are no distinctions
in the ultimate state, if everything and everyone is 'lost'
in God, and even God himself is 'lost' in the One, the
absolute, non-dual Being. Of course, they are 'lost' in
one sense; they are lost to their finite, separate mode of
being and to all conceptual distinctions, but they are
'found' in their eternal Truth, their being in the Word.
God himself remains eternally Creator; all created
beings come forth eternally in his Word. They are known
and willed, each in its particularity, as finite expressions
of his infinite being. In his Word they stand in eternal
relationship with him, for though there is no 'duality',
there is relationship in the Godhead. The Father knows
himself and all things eternally 'without duality' in his

Word, and his Spirit is poured out in love upon the Word, the Son, and upon all men in him. There is no 'duality' here, no 'superimposition' on the One. All is one infinite Being, Knowledge and Bliss, being in pure consciousness of unending bliss. Each created being participates in this one Being, this one Consciousness, this one Bliss of love, because the one Word expresses himself in them, the one Spirit unites them in love. This is our destiny, to participate in that one consciousness of the Word, to love with the one love of that blissful Spirit.

Every creature is a capacity for God, a capacity which God alone can fulfil. In itself it is nothing; it is a want of being, a desire of being, a need for being; it has no being in itself. It is this lack of being which distinguishes the creature – from the highest angel to the grain of sand – from God. God is Being itself, the Fullness of being in whom there is no lack of being, no unfulfilled capacity at all. 'I am he who is,' as the Lord said to Catherine of Siena, 'you are she who is not.' This is the mystery of creation, this element of not-being, this absence of being; this is *maya*, 'an appearance of being, without origin, inexpressible in terms of being as of not-being'.[4] It is not absolute not-being, absolute nothing, since it is a capacity for being, yet this capacity has no being in itself. The being of the creature is wholly from God; but the creature is not God because of this lack of being, this limitation of being. The creature is a limited, finite being in which the infinite being of God is reflected. It·is as though the one divine light were received into each of these 'capacities', each reflecting it in its own way and breaking it up into innumerable colours, each a unique reflection of the one light. The one Word reflects itself in each of these energies, giving to each its own proper being, but remaining unchanged in itself. The Spirit –

the divine Sakti – fills each of these capacities with its infinite energy and pervades the whole creation to the furthest reaches of matter – yet its energy remains ever the same. 'That [the divine Being] is full; this [the creation] is full; take the full [the creation] from the full [the divine] and the full remains.'[5]

SIX

Sin and Redemption

But where does sin and evil come into this picture? Each created being reflects the divine light, is moved by the divine energy. In material things, in plants and animals, the divine light is reflected unconsciously, the divine energy is present in the form of blind impulse and instinct – yet it is this divine light which shines in the stars, and irradiates the earth with its precious stones, its flowers and butterflies and birds and animal forms; it is the divine energy which moves the galaxies and this earth and the solar system, and energizes the atoms and molecules and living cells from which this earth is constructed. But in man the divine life is received into a conscious capacity, it is reflected in an intelligence like its own. The divine energy is received in a will, a capacity for action, which is illuminated by the intelligence and is therefore free. We can recognize the divine light and energy in us and recognize our own nothingness, our total dependence on the divine Being. But we can also seek to appropriate the divine light, to make ourselves the judge and master, to act as though our power came from ourselves. This is original sin, this is the great illusion. This is what is always happening in all of us. It is then that we become imprisoned in this world of space and time and lose the vision of eternity. It is then that we imagine ourselves to be material bodies subject to the inevitable laws of matter and destined to death, and lose our hope of immortality. It is then that each becomes centred on himself and in conflict with his

neighbour and forgets his real Self and his solidarity
with all men.

Sin is the refusal to recognize our own nothingness —
that in ourselves we are a mere want, a need, a desire.
Not only have we nothing, but we are nothing of ourselves. Our very existence is from another. To recognize
this is truth and life. Then we begin to live in God and
through God and for God. Then God begins to live in us.
To allow God to live in us, to think in us, to act in us,
this is our need, our capacity. Each of us is a unique
capacity for God. God creates this capacity in order that
he may communicate himself to us. An ant, a flea, a
mosquito, each is a unique capacity for God, a unique
manifestation of the divine life. But they receive the
divine life passively, each enclosed in its own nature.
But we have the capacity to respond to the divine life,
our capacity to receive actually grows with the receiving.
But it must be received without appropriation. Everything has to be received from God and returned to God,
not appropriated. This is the systole and the diastole of
the divine life. The divine life pours out from God over
the whole creation and returns again to him — and yet,
of course, there is no movement in God. The effect of
receiving and returning is found in the creature and is a
reflection of the eternal act of love in God, by which the
love of the Father goes out to the Son and returns in the
Holy Spirit.

Each of us comes forth from God in the Word and
stands before him, unique in his own nature, in his own
particular being, a unique expression of the divine
Being; and each of us has to return to God in the Holy
Spirit, in a movement of love by which we surrender
ourselves to God, allow God to possess us. Our temptation is to stand upon our own dignity, to centre on our-

selves and refuse that movement of return, of self-surrender. Sin is a failure of love, a failure to respond to the movement of grace which is ever drawing us out of ourselves into the divine life. When we refuse to respond, to acknowledge our nothingness and need, then we close in on ourselves, we become separated from God and eternal life and see ourselves as isolated selves, each shut up in our own existence and in conflict with others, alienated from our real Self, living in a world of illusion.

Suffering and death are the effect of sin. Suffering arises because we are shut up in our selves and experience our own limitations. If we were surrendered to God, we would not suffer. The physical pain might be there, even mental pain, but the soul in its depths, in its ground, would be at peace. This was the nature of the suffering of Christ on the cross. He suffered the physical pain and the mental pain which are the effect of sin, but he surrendered his soul to God and thereby redeemed the world. Suffering and death became a sacrament, a means of entry into the divine life. Death is only evil when it is seen from the point of view of the ego – the ego which is enclosed in itself and refuses to die, to surrender itself to God. When the self is surrendered to God, then death becomes a sacrament; it is simply the passage into eternal life.

What about the suffering of animals? An animal experiences pain, but it does not really suffer, because suffering is the result of a reflective consciousness. Pain is a physical reaction, suffering is due to conscious reflection on it. An animal, like a child who has not yet reached reflective consciousness, is aware of the pain, but it does not reflect upon it. It is human consciousness which brings misery into the world, and that because human consciousness has become self-centred. Even primitive man suffered very little in comparison with modern man, because his powers of reflection were less developed and he lived spontaneously from the Self. It is only in modern man that the problem of suffering has become acute. He has cut himself off from the Self, with its awareness of transcendent Reality, and concentrated his powers of reflective consciousness on his ego and its environment, and so is exposed to all the terrors of a self-centred consciousness, alienated from God and nature. But the remedy is also there. A reflective consciousness can always turn back from the ego and rediscover the Self, and the more acute the self-consciousness, the more profound can be its Self-realization.

The reflective consciousness is the source of all sin and misery, but it is also the source of salvation. Primitive man, like the child and the animal, lived spontaneously from the Self, from the Source of being. He was one with nature, obeying her laws spontaneously, and therefore at peace with himself. He had not yet learned to distinguish himself as an individual; he thought and felt as a member of a tribe, as part of a whole. Pain and death were there, but they were not reflected on and therefore they caused no break in his consciousness. Nature was not something external to himself but something within, a world of spirits with which he was in constant communion. The spirits of the dead, of the ancestors, were inhabitants of this same world. There was no barrier between the waking and the dream state; in the dream state the world of spirits came closer and he could commune with it. It was not so much he who thought (for thought is a product of the reflective consciousness), as nature who reflected herself in him. The one Self, the Spirit, reflected itself in nature and the human consciousness. It was a blissful state of innocence – the original paradise. Man was naked and unashamed. Sex was the spontaneous movement of nature in him and produced no feeling of shame. His consciousness was still undivided, the consciousness of the one Self. But the germ of self-consciousness was there. He could allow the Self to reflect itself in him, so as to live in its light, but he could also reflect upon himself, upon his ego, and know himself as an isolated individual, separated from nature and from his fellow-men and from his Ground in the Self.

Modern man has experienced this isolation, this alienation, more than any man in history. All the ancient cultures, the Egyptian and Babylonian, the Persian, the Indian and the Chinese, not to mention the African and Australian and American Indian, sought to preserve this integrity of man, to keep him in touch with the eternal Reality. The Greeks were the first to emancipate themselves from this eternal Law, to develop a rational consciousness, which made man the measure of all things. But with the Greek this divorce of the rational consciousness was only in germ; his great philosophers, Plato and Aristotle, the Stoics and Plotinus, kept him in touch with the Truth. It was only at the Renaissance that the movement towards the emancipation of man from the universal Law, from the sacred order of truth and morality, really took hold. Then the reflective consciousness turned away from the eternal light of Truth and began to concentrate on man and nature. The marvels of modern science and technology, the transformation of the world and of human society, which we have witnessed, are the fruits of this reflective consciousness centred on man and nature. But the cost of it has been the alienation of man from his true Self, from the Ground of being, of truth and morality, and now he is exposed to all the destructive forces which this has released. Yet the reflective consciousness can always turn back. Instead of concentrating on man and nature and centring on the ego, it can turn back to their source and find the Self. This is conversion, *metanoia* – the discovery of the real Self, of eternal life.

Of course to know the Self is to know man and nature, but it is to know them not dispersed in space and time and cut off from reality, but in their integrity and unity as an organic whole, every part related to every other, every point reflecting the whole. But what about all the conflict in nature, one animal preying on another, the immeasurable suffering in human life? Conflict and suffering are part of the pattern of things evolving in space and time. They belong to the world of becoming, of change and decay. The misery of human suffering lies in the fact that our consciousness is divided. We experience the world and ourselves in their dispersion in time and space, in the flux of becoming. But if we could see with an undivided consciousness, we should know the world and ourselves not in the process of becoming but in the achievement of being, not as separate parts but as an organic whole. The whole process of change, of evolution, would be there, but known not in its partial, divided, transient state, but in its undivided being, its total reality. When Christ was hanging on the cross, he experienced the pain of the whole world from the beginning to the end of time, because he experienced it in the Word, which is before all things and in all things and above all things. By this suffering the pain of the world was reconciled with God, brought into the unity of the divine life.

When Christ 'descended into hell', he went down into the depths of the unconscious. In every man the whole

creation is present – man is the microcosm of the macro-
cosm. He goes through all the stages of evolution, from
first matter to human consciousness. But for most of us
this all lies buried in the unconscious. Christ opened up
the depths of the unconscious to divine consciousness.
He redeemed the whole creation by opening it to the
divine life, the life of the Word, which filled his human
consciousness. It is said that every man recapitulates in
the womb not only all the stages of the evolution of
matter but also all the stages of the evolution of human
consciousness. In each of us Adam – mankind – is
present in the unconscious and we bear within us the
history of humanity. Perhaps this may be the meaning
of the saying that the Buddha at his enlightenment
experienced all his former 'births'. So also Christ must
have experienced in himself the history of humanity, not
unconsciously but consciously. He took upon himself the
sin and suffering of the whole world; he recapitulated all
its stages and brought it up into the consciousness of the
Word. This is the meaning of redemption. Each of us
was 'in Christ' on the cross, just as each of us was in
Adam when he sinned. We bear the sin of Adam in us –
the sin of man – but in Christ our human consciousness
has been opened to the divine. For most of us this still
lies buried in the unconscious – both our sin and our
redemption – but as we wake to the consciousness of sin,
so we wake to the consciousness of redemption. We are
fully redeemed only when our human consciousness,
with all that was formerly buried in the unconscious, is
possessed by the divine consciousness, and we know ourselves and humanity and the universe in the light of the
Word.

There is no such thing as individual salvation. We are
saved as members of a Body, of an organic whole, of man

and the universe. Just as we are 'born in sin', as members of a fallen humanity, so we are born in Christ, as members of his Body, of redeemed mankind. 'As in Adam all die, so also in Christ shall all be made alive.'[1] Each of us has to work out his salvation within the pattern of the whole. No one sins in isolation, no one suffers in isolation, no one is redeemed in isolation, no one is glorified in isolation. It is only when we see the sufferings of the world, the inequalities of the world, the injustices of the world, within this pattern of the whole, in their relation to the eternal order, 'in Christ', that we shall see their meaning and their justification. 'God was in Christ reconciling the world to himself.'[2] This will only be manifested in the Parousia, when the Son 'delivers the kingdom to God the Father', the process of evolution will be completed, and all things will be recapitulated in Christ, 'that God may be everything to everyone'.[3]

All men are included in this plan of salvation: it is mankind as a whole which is redeemed. As Gregory of Nyssa said: 'All men from the first man to the last man are but one image of him who is.' Christ is the image of God and in him is found the image of all mankind. But does that mean that all men are saved? It would be nice to think so, but man's freedom remains. Freedom is the power to assent to the divine life within us, to grow into the divine consciousness, but it is also the power to reject the divine life, to centre on the self, and to be enclosed in this world of becoming. But this world, considered apart from the divine life which is its ground, is an illusory world, it has no real being. To withdraw from the divine is therefore to retreat into unreality. It is to fail to achieve being. This would be hell – to be finally cut off from Life and Truth and Reality, to be lost in a total illusion – the outer darkness, outside being.

Hell is the state of a being without love. The world was created by love and for love. For love is self-communication. There is a power of self-communication in the divine Being by which it seeks to communicate itself to others. The world came into being as a result of this urge to self-communication in God, and every creature is moved by love. Every creature receives its being from the love of God and is urged to communicate itself in love. Love is present in the first elements of matter and in the living cell, building up the world by this process of attraction and self-communication. As Empedocles said, love and strife are the two forces which move the universe. In other creatures they are unconscious, but in us they become conscious. We can choose to love, to give ourselves to others and finally to Love itself, which is drawing us to itself. But we can also reject this movement of love; we can turn our love, the driving force of our nature, on ourselves and become centres not of love but of strife. Self-love is the root of all sin and it is deep in us all. Our whole life is a battle between these two forces, love of God, the Infinite, the Eternal, the Transcendent, for which we were made, or for ourselves – not for our true Self, which is found in God, but for our ego, the self which tries to attract all love to itself and refuses to surrender itself. We have to choose, as St Augustine said, between love of God to the contempt of self – the individual, divided self – and love of self to the contempt of God.

SEVEN

The Cosmic Powers

But are there beings other than ourselves which have this power of choice? In every religious tradition there is a belief in a world of spirits above man, the gods of the Greeks and Romans, the 'devas' of Hinduism, the 'asuras' of Zoroastrianism, the angels of the Jewish-Christian tradition. These are the 'powers' of nature. It is an illusion to imagine, as our scientific education teaches us to do, that there is any such thing as a merely material world. Matter as we conceive it is an abstraction from the total reality of being. The organization of matter, with its mathematical precision, is clearly the work of an intelligence, and the angels in the Islamic as well as in the Christian tradition have always been conceived of as 'intelligences'. They are the 'cosmic powers' of St Paul, the forces at work in the evolution of the cosmos and also of humanity. Between the physical world as we know it, as observed by science, and the spiritual world, the world of divine reality, there is a 'psychic' or 'astral' world. Hindu tradition distinguishes between gross senses and subtle senses on the one hand, and gross matter and subtle matter on the other. These subtle senses are present in all men but in most people today they are not developed. Our scientific habit of mind has taught us to concentrate on gross matter and its rational analysis, so that the subtle senses, with their intuitive perception, have become atrophied. But the evidence accumulates continually, both in past history and in present experience, of the existence of this 'psychic' world, the world of 'extra-sensory perception', of dream and vision, of telepathy and telekinesis, of spiritual healing and control of the mind over the body. When Christ performed his miracles of walking on the water and stilling the storm, of multiplying bread and changing water into wine, of healing the sick and 'casting out devils', of foreseeing the future, and finally of rising from the dead, he was demonstrating not merely the power of God but the powers latent in human nature, powers which man, when freed from sin and transformed by the indwelling Spirit, is destined to realize. These powers, or *siddhis*, have a long history in India and are the recognized effect of the more advanced practice of Yoga.

Are these cosmic powers good or evil? In themselves they are good: they are created by God, manifestations of the divine Sakti. The stellar universe, with its millions of suns and stars, travelling at immense speed, radiating heat and light, is a reflection in space and time of these angelic hosts. So also is the earth, with its millions of living things, the biosphere, reflecting the heat and light of the sun. Everywhere there are angels present – pure intelligences, ordering the movements of the stars, organizing the growth of living things from the earth. There are angels also present in human life, watching over the destiny both of nations and individuals. But all these angels are not good. The forces of conflict in nature and in man are demonic powers. When the angel is subject to the law of God and reflects the divine light, then it becomes the instrument of God in the ordering of the universe. But when it turns and centres on itself, making itself its own law, then it becomes a power of strife and disorder. The destructive forces in nature and the disintegrating forces in the human psyche are demonic powers which have become separated from

God, from the universal order. A Hitler or a Stalin is a man possessed by these demonic powers, and so in different degrees are all who do evil. We none of us escape the influence both of the angelic and the demonic powers working in the unconscious. Those who imagine themselves to be emancipated from such 'superstitions' are most firmly in their power. The rational mind, emancipated from any higher law and imagining itself to be detached, impartial, objective, and all the rest – the mind of the scholar and the scientist – is always exposed to these demonic influences. We are parts of a cosmic whole and no one can escape its laws. Either we must be governed by the universal Law, the eternal Reason, or we shall be governed by demonic forces. This is why men of genius who lack 'wisdom', like Luther and Calvin, Voltaire and Rousseau, Marx and Freud, release such incalculable forces of evil.

These demonic forces are, of course, also present in the Church. Immediately after Christ had said to Peter: 'You are Peter, and on this rock I will build my church, and the powers of death shall not prevail against it', he turned on him and said: 'Get behind me, Satan!'[1] Christ and Satan are always present in the Church as in the world, and the conflict will go on to the end of time. The only assurance we have is that 'the powers of death' will not finally prevail. It is the same with all religions. In Hinduism, Buddhism, Islam, good and evil – the angelic and the demonic powers – are always present. In this sphere of 'dualities' there is no final victory. But in each religion the divine Truth is also present – the One above all duality, the Infinite, the Eternal. Every religion, from the most primitive to the most advanced, is a pathway to this One. To realize the One above the dualities, to know the Self, is the goal of all religion.

EIGHT

The Mystery of Love

Of this one Reality it has been said: 'There has always been an eternally abiding Reality. The realm of Reality [*dharma-dhatu*] abides for ever, whether a Tathagata [that is, a Buddha] appears in the world or not. So does the Realness [*dharmata*] of all things eternally abide: so does the supreme Being [*paramartha*] abide and keep its order. What has been realized by myself [the Buddha] and all the Tathagatas [Buddhas] is this Body of Reality [*dharmakaya*], the eternally abiding self-orderliness of reality, the suchness [*tathata*] of things, the nature [*bhutata*] of things, noble Wisdom which is Truth itself. The sun radiates its splendour on all alike: in like manner do the Tathagatas [Buddhas] radiate the truth of noble Wisdom without recourse to words and on all alike.'[1] This is the Truth proclaimed by Buddhism, a Truth which cannot properly be expressed in words but has to be realized within.

This one Truth, which cannot be expressed, is present in all religion, making itself known, communicating itself by signs. The myths and rituals of primitive religion, the doctrines and sacraments of the more advanced, are all signs of this eternal Truth, reflected in the conscious-ness of man. Each religion manifests some aspect of this one Reality, creates a system of symbols by which this Truth may be known, this Reality experienced. In this sense Christ is the symbol of God; in making known the one, transcendent Truth, he makes present the one absolute Reality by his words and actions. The Word of

God is that Truth itself, that eternal Reality, coming
forth from the Father, the abyss of Being, the unmani-
fested One, and communicating the bliss of being, the
Spirit of love. In Jesus of Nazareth that Word became
flesh, manifesting the Father in a human form, communicating the Spirit to his disciples. But that human
form is conditioned by space and time. It came into
existence at a particular time, at a particular place. It
was conditioned by the heredity of a particular people,
physically and mentally. Jesus had the physical and
mental characteristics of a Jew. He could only express
himself in Aramaic; he could only think of himself and
of God in terms of the Jewish scriptures. Even though he
lived in the Graeco-Roman world, he had no knowledge
of Latin or Greek, much less of Sanskrit or Chinese. Yet
in the depth of his soul, in the ground of his being,
beyond words and thoughts, he knew himself to be the
Word of God, one with the Father and the Holy Spirit.
He experienced himself in his eternal being, coming
forth from the Father, communicating in the bliss of the
Spirit.

This is what is unique in the teaching of Jesus. He
knew himself in the eternal Ground of being, as the
Buddha had done, as the seers of the Upanishads had
done. He knew himself as manifesting this eternal Truth
in time, as communicating the bliss of the supreme
Spirit to the world. But he also knew himself as the
eternal manifestation of the Father, as communicating
eternally in the bliss of the Spirit. His was an experience
of personal relationship. The abyss of Being, the divine
Darkness, the One beyond being, revealed itself to him
as Father, and the bliss of the Supreme, the divine
ananda, revealed itself to him as the Spirit of love,
eternally welling up from the depths of the Godhead and

eternally returning to its source. Reality itself is this eternal procession of self-manifestation, of self-knowledge, and this eternal overflow of bliss, this eternal self-giving in love. This is what is happening in each one of us, if we could only know ourselves. We are for ever coming forth from the Father into the light of self-knowledge, for ever returning to the Father in the bliss of love. All our knowledge in this world and all our striving for love is only a pale reflection of this everlasting wisdom and love.

If we could go down into the depths of any being, a grain of sand, a leaf, a flower, we should come upon this eternal mystery. Beyond the molecules and atoms, beyond the protons and electrons, beyond the living cell with its genes and chromosomes, there is an energy, a force of life, which is continually welling up from the abyss of being in the Father, continually springing up into the light of the Word, continually flowing back to its source in the bliss of love. The divine Saccidananda, the Holy Trinity, lies at the heart of every creature. As the Upanishad says: 'The Self, smaller than the small, greater than the great, is hidden in the heart of every creature. A man who is free from desires and free from grief sees the majesty of the Self by the grace of the Creator.'[2] This mystery is hidden in the heart of every man, but we fail to see it: we are turned in on ourselves and not touched by 'the grace of the Creator'. But there are some in all ages and in all times who wake to this knowledge, who know the Truth. These are the seers, the prophets, the wise men. The Buddha was such an enlightened one, and so were the seers of the Upanishads, so were Lao Tzu and Zoroaster, so were the Hebrew prophets, so were Plato and Plotinus, so were the Sufi mystics. In every religion, and in every country this mystery has been made known. Each approaches it from a different point of view, each expresses it in different terms, but in all the mystery is the same, the one eternal Truth manifesting itself in space and time, the one unchanging Light reflecting itself in human consciousness. Even those who reject the Truth and deny the Mystery, the atheist and the unbeliever, yet bear witness to it. For the one Truth is present in every partial truth, the one Spirit is present in every movement of love.

Why is it, then, that mankind remains shut up in this world of partial truths, of frustrated love? Sankara says that it is due to 'ignorance' – to *avidya*. The soul has lost the knowledge of the One and is caught in the net of *maya*, of illusion. But what is the cause of *maya*, he cannot explain. The Buddha comes near to the truth when he says that clinging to the self, the desire for a separate existence, is the root of evil. So also a Muslim tradition says: 'Your own existence is your greatest sin' – that is, your separate existence apart from the Self. But the root cause both of 'ignorance' and of self-love is sin. It is a movement of the free will turning away from God, from the Truth, and rejecting Love, refusing the self-surrender which Love demands. In Jesus a man was found who turned back to God, who knew the Truth and who surrendered himself to Love in a total self-giving. At this moment in space and time the Truth was manifested in a love of total self-surrender. This is the final revelation of the mystery, the Father revealing his Self to the world and communicating his Spirit, and this Self and this Spirit are Love.

In other words, the ultimate Mystery of being, the ultimate Truth, is Love. This is the essential structure of reality. When Dante spoke of the 'love which moves the sun and the other stars', he was not using a metaphor, he was describing the nature of reality. There is in Being an infinite desire to give itself in love and this gift of Self in love is for ever answered by a return of love. The Father gives himself in love to the Son, who is the very form, the expression, of his love, and this love returns to the Father in the Holy Spirit, who unites Father and Son in the eternal embrace of love. Love giving itself, losing itself and finding itself in love, and Love returning to itself, giving itself back in love – this is the eternal pattern of the universe. Every creature in the depth of its being is a desire, a longing for Love, and is drawn by Love to give itself in love. This is its coming into being, this response to the drawing of Love. At the same time it is being continually drawn to give itself in love, to surrender to the attraction of Love, and so the rhythm of the universe is created. The nucleus throws out its protons and electrons and they circle round it, held by the attraction of Love. The sun throws out its planets and they circle round it, held by the same attraction. The cell divides and then again unites, building up the body in love. It is the same with sexual love. The male is drawn to give himself in love to the female, and the female is drawn to give herself back in love to the male. There is a continual dance of love, a continual going and returning. Ultimately it is the one Love giving itself continually so as to create this form and that form, building up the universe of stars and atoms and living cells, and then drawing everything back to itself; everything coming into being in the Word as an expression of love, and everything returning to the Father, to the Source, in the love of the Spirit.

Every human being has in his heart this desire to love and to be loved. It is the very structure of his being. It is built into the cells of his body and is the deepest instinct in his soul. A child lives and grows by love. This is why a child who is deprived of love in its infancy suffers an irremediable loss. Fear and sorrow, anger and hatred, are only expressions of frustrated love. But the trouble is that there is always something selfish in human love. The desire to be loved, to possess love for one's self is too strong and the will to give to others is too weak. This is the effect of sin. Sin is always the refusal to love, or rather the rejection of the rhythm of love, the desire to get and not to give. The mother wants to possess the child's love and not just to take it as it comes. The child wants to possess the mother's love and not to respond to a love which would draw it out of itself. It is the same in sexual love: the man wants to possess the woman, the woman wants to possess the man. We all keep falling back on self-love. But real love is always response to the love of another, a self-giving with no thought of return. We can only receive in so far as we are willing to give. Ultimately, it is always the love of God which is drawing us through every human love, drawing us to give ourselves back in return for the love we have received. That is why all love is holy, from the love of atoms or of insects to the love of man. It is always a reflection of the love of God.

This is why sex is holy. The desire of union is the reflection in us of the love of the Holy Trinity. May we not say that the Holy Spirit is feminine? It is the eternal Wisdom, which in Hebrew, Greek and Latin is always feminine, the divine Sophia. The Holy Spirit is immanent in all creation. It is the love which draws the Father to create, to conceive the whole creation in his Son. In Hindu tradition the world comes into being as the result of the union of Siva and Sakti, the divine consciousness uniting with the divine power. This is why the lingam and the yoni[3] are sacred in India. They are symbols of

Siva and Sakti, of Purusha and Prakriti;[4] every human marriage reflects this divine marriage, is a symbol of the marriage of heaven and earth. Sexual love is never complete on the physical plàne – it has to pass beyond to the psychic and the spiritual, to penetrate the 'three worlds'. The union of bodies is a sign, or a sacrament, of the union of souls: it has no meaning unless it leads to psychic, that is emotional and imaginative, fulfilment. But psychic fulfilment in turn is a sign and expression of a deeper spiritual fulfilment. Sexual experience when it is complete engages the depth of the soul, it opens upon the divine, it unites man, that is man and woman in one, with God. This is why love is so demanding and can be so tragic. If it turns back from the divine and tries to satisfy itself with the psychic or the physical, it becomes frustrated.

To confine love to the psychic or physical plane is to profane it: it is literally to put it 'outside the temple'. This is why among all people marriage has always had a solemn and sacred character. This is what lies behind the custom of the devadasi in India – the girl who is consecrated to God in the temple – and the fertility rites of the ancient world. Love is the basic pattern of the universe and by sexual union man and woman enter into communion with the divine. It restores the original harmony of the universe. Man and woman are restored to their original unity, they become one with the cosmic order and are united to God. For many people today sex is the one means of opening to the divine, to the world of transcendent mystery. But, of course, it is fatally easy to miss its transcendent character, to make it 'profane', and then it becomes demonic. This is a repetition of original sin, a refusal to surrender to the divine in love and so achieve a sacramental union; to turn back instead on the

self and make it a means of self-gratification, and so
become a slave of the demon, the demonic power which
is love separated from God.

Sex, then, is the sacrament of love. It is the means
which nature has contrived for the expression of love,
first in the plant and animal world, then in man. It is
the outward and visible sign of the mystery of love, which
lies at the heart of the universe. But it belongs essentially
to this world of signs and appearances; it is the shadow
of love, and has therefore always to be transcended. Not
only the physical expression of love, but also the psychic
division of man into male and female, are stages in the
evolution of man, through which we have to pass before
we can realize the mystery of love. Every man and
woman is both male and female. The division of the sexes
is the means which nature has contrived for developing
these characteristics in separation, so that they may
eventually be reunited. The man has to find his feminine
side in the woman, and the woman her masculine side in
the man. Then only is human nature fully achieved,
where the marriage of the male and the female has taken
place in each person. The exterior marriage is for the
sake of the interior marriage, in which man and woman
recover their original unity. In heaven, we are told, there
is neither marrying nor giving in marriage, and in Christ
there is neither male nor female. So also the god Siva
unites in himself the male and the female; in the final
state Siva and Sakti are one.

The virgin birth of Jesus is a sign of the emergence of
the new man, a further stage in the evolution of humanity. It marks the transcendence of sexuality, the
achievement of human perfection. The new man is not
born by sexual generation – 'not of blood nor of the will
of the flesh nor of the will of man, but of God'.[5] This is

achieved because a woman is found who can make the total surrender of herself in love. What human love strives imperfectly to achieve through sex and marriage is here accomplished by divine Love. The mystery of love which is at work in the whole creation, in the stars and atoms, plants and animals and men, here achieved its consummation. In Mary man is married to God; the male and the female unite in one person in an interior marriage and the new man is born. This is the mystery which has to be accomplished in us. Every man and woman has to undergo this virgin birth, to be married to God. In other words, beyond our physical and psychic being we have to discover our spiritual being, our eternal ground, and there the mystery of love is fulfilled. Some may come to this interior marriage by way of exterior marriage, others are called by the way of virginity, but all alike have to experience the virgin birth, the marriage with God, before they can reach maturity. As the Upanishad says: 'Not for the sake of the husband is the husband dear, but for the sake of the Self [the Spirit, the eternal in man]. Not for the sake of the wife is the wife dear, but for the sake of the Self [the Spirit, the eternal].'[6]

The myth of the virgin birth is universal and represents one of the profoundest aspirations of humanity. The instinct of love in our nature can never be satisfied with anything less than God, that is with the Infinite. Human marriage is but a shadow and a symbol of the spiritual marriage which has to take place in the 'cave of the heart'. This is the return to the womb, the marriage with the mother, which depth psychology has discovered to be a basic human desire. Man and woman were once whole and undivided, enclosed in the womb of nature, in the paradise of God, and man has ever since suffered from the nostalgia for paradise, the desire for that perfect unity. But this unity cannot be realized in the flesh: an angel with a flaming sword stands in the way, preventing the return. Man has to advance through the desert of this world, always seeking the Promised Land, the 'city which has foundations, whose builder and maker is God'.[7] Marriage, like all other earthly pleasures and achievements, is only a temporary resting-place, a foretaste of the fulfilment of love which he seeks. The secular city is only a stage on the path of evolution, and every civilization is destined to pass away. In ancient Indian society there were four *ashramas*, or stages of life. The first was that of the *brahmachari*, the student or 'seeker of God', who has to acquire the knowledge necessary both for life in this world and for that which is to come. The next stage is that of the householder, who raises a family and builds up the city and the State. But this is followed by that of the *vanaprastha* and the *sannyasi*, retirement to the forest and finally renunciation of the world to prepare for 'liberation'.

This is the basic pattern of human society, as was realized in one way or another in all the ancient world. The modern world has lost this orientation towards a transcendent state. It has stopped at the second *ashrama* and has no place for the *vanaprastha* and the *sannyasi* – that is, it has no place for the monk. Yet the monk, or *sannyasi*, is essential for the well-being of the State. He keeps before it the goal of transcendence, without which secular life loses its meaning. In ancient India there were four 'ends' of life, pleasure (*kama*), wealth (*artha*), duty (*dharma*) and liberation (*moksha*). The modern world recognizes the first three but has lost sight of the last, yet without this goal of final liberation, of ultimate transcendence, all the other goals lead to frustration. Again, in ancient India there were four castes – the Brahmin or priest, the *kshatriya*, the warrior or ruler, the *vaisya*, the merchant or farmer, and the *sudra*, the worker. The modern world has a place for the worker, for the merchant or industrialist, and for the soldier or the politician, but it has no place for the Brahmin or priest. Yet it is the priest who keeps the link with the Transcendent, with the ultimate meaning of life.

NINE

The Ultimate Truth

The essential need is to recover this sense of a transcendent Reality, of an ultimate Truth. Science and technology are of no assistance in this. The more we explore the physical universe and the further we extend our control over it, the further we move from the Centre in which this truth is known. The social sciences are of no help: they also only study the external phenomena, they never reach the root of human personality, they never answer the question, what is man? The way to the Truth is not that of progress but that of return. There can be no constant progress in the knowledge of the Truth. There is only a constant movement of return, of *metanoia*, of turning back. There can only be a constant striving to return to the Source, to the Origin, to what the Chinese call the 'uncarved block'. 'Unless you turn and become like children, you will never enter the kingdom of heaven.'[1] Humility, simplicity, purity of heart, these are the pathway to Truth. They lead to knowledge of the Self, of the Centre, of the One. When this knowledge has been acquired, then all other knowledge follows. Science and technology, philosophy and sociology, all flow from this source; but when they forget their source, they lose their meaning and lead to disaster.

This is the root cause of the failure of modern civilization. It has lost touch with the Centre, the Ground of reality and truth, and therefore it is doomed to destruction. Its breakdown may come sooner or later; it may take place within the next thirty years, or, like the Roman Empire, it may break up gradually over a period of two or three hundred years, but nothing can now save it. It is not that science and technology and the whole economic and political development of humanity today is wrong in itself. On the contrary, every element which goes to make up modern civilization has a value in itself. Science, in the sense of the rational study of the physical universe, including the body of man, and technology, in the sense of the application of this knowledge to the control of the forces of nature for the benefit of man, are intrinsically good. So also humanism, in the sense of respect for the human person, of the recognition of the rights of man, of liberty, equality and fraternity – such humanism is intrinsically good but it has been vitiated from the beginning by the rejection of the eternal Wisdom, of the ultimate Ground of truth and morality. What is intrinsically evil is the pretence that this world has being in itself, that the physical world presented to our senses, which is the object of science, is reality. What is sinful is the belief that man is independent of any transcendent reality and can control the universe – or at least as much as he can bring under his control – for his own purposes. This is the 'world' which is judged and condemned in the Gospel, the world which sets itself up as independent of God and attempts to deify man. This is the world which is *maya*, the product of *avidya*, of ignorance, of a spiritual blindness which has lost touch with reality. As the *Katha* Upanishad says: 'Abiding in the midst of ignorance, thinking themselves wise and learned, fools go aimlessly hither and thither, like blind led by the blind. What lies beyond this life never shines for those who are childish or careless or deluded by wealth. "This is the only world", they say –

"there is no other"; and so they go from death to death.'[2]

The great illusion is to think that the world of the senses is the real world, whereas it is obvious that it can never be more than an abstraction from the total reality. That portion of reality which is reflected through our senses is only a fraction of the whole. No matter how far the range of the senses is extended through the telescope or the microscope, it can never touch more than one aspect of reality. But it is no less an illusion to think that the world of reason is the real world. All the constructions of mathematical reason on the basis of the senses, all the grandiose systems of philosophy based on sense and reason, are only the reflection in the human mind of a Reality which always transcends it. Only when we come to the intuitions of the great prophets and seers which are the basis of religion do we begin to touch Reality itself, and even then this one Reality is still reflected through a human medium. The Rig-Veda, together with the Upanishads and the Gita, the Buddhist Sutras, the Zend-Avesta, the Koran, the Old and the New Testaments, all alike reflect this one Truth in different human terms. All alike are conditioned by history and circumstance, but all derive from the one Source and all alike point to the one Reality.

TEN

The One Spirit in All Religion

The function of comparative religion is to discern this essential Truth, this divine Mystery beyond speech and thought, in the language-forms and thought-forms of each religious tradition, from the most primitive tribal traditions to the most advanced world religions. In each tradition the one divine Reality, the one eternal Truth, is present, but it is hidden under symbols, symbols of word and gesture, of ritual and dance and song, of poetry and music, art and architecture, of custom and convention, of law and morality, of philosophy and theology. Always the divine Mystery is hidden under a veil, but each revelation (or 'unveiling') unveils some aspect of the one Truth, or, if you like, the veil becomes thinner at a certain point. The Semitic religions, Judaism and Islam, reveal the transcendent aspect of the divine Mystery with incomparable power. The oriental religions reveal the divine Immanence with immeasurable depth. Yet in each the opposite aspect is contained, though in a more hidden way. We have to try to discover the inner relationship between these different aspects of Truth and unite them in ourselves. I have to be a Hindu, a Buddhist, a Jain, a Parsee, a Sikh, a Muslim, and a Jew, as well as a Christian, if I am to know the Truth and to find the point of reconciliation in all religion.

Every religion as long as it continues to live is in a state of evolution. We can watch the process in the development of Hinduism from the original Aryan religion of the Rig-Veda, through the Brahmanas and Upanishads and the Bhagavad-Gita, gradually absorbing elements from the ancient Dravidian religion, learning from Buddhism, later from Islam, and finally from Christianity. We can see Buddhism evolving from the simple, primitive cult of the Hinayana to the vast complexity of the Mahayana, absorbing innumerable elements from Hinduism, yet always giving them a new and distinctive character, and adopting ever new forms as it spreads through China, Tibet and Japan. We can see the primitive Arabian religion of the Koran evolving through its contact with the Syrian and Persian cultures and developing a mystical doctrine through direct contact with Hinduism. As for Judaism, we can watch its evolution in the Old Testament itself from a primitive tribal religion to the universalism of the prophets, learning from Egypt and Babylonia and Persia and Greece and developing new characteristics through its dispersion in the gentile world, yet always conditioned by its past and remaining true to its original revelation. In each tradition the one divine Truth receives a particular mould to which it remains true throughout its evolution.

The need is to discern in each religion the character of this primitive mould. Often it can be summed up in a single word. For Hinduism it is Brahman, the 'one without a second', the Infinite, the Eternal, Saccidananda – Being, Knowledge, Bliss. In Hinduism everything refers back to this one, unspeakable Mystery. In Buddhism it is Nirvana, the cessation of being, the blowing out of the fire of life, the state beyond consciousness, the emptiness in which all fullness is contained. It is the negative aspect of the divine Mystery. In Islam, it is Islam itself, the 'surrender' to Allah, the beneficent, the merciful, the one Truth and Reality in its absolute transcendence. In

Judaism it is Yahweh, the Holy One of Israel, the Eternal in his self-manifestation in history, the divine Mystery hidden in clouds and darkness, yet ever close to the heart of man.

What of Christianity? It is the revelation of the divine Mystery in the person of Christ. The one, eternal Truth, which cannot be uttered, which cannot be known, is 'symbolized' in the life and death and resurrection of Jesus of Nazareth. At this point in history the veil is pierced, the Mystery shines through. At the resurrection of Jesus, human nature was taken up into the divine, time was taken up into eternity. Yet these are only phrases we use to express the inexpressible. It is not by word or thought but by meditation on the Mystery that we can pierce the veil. This is where all human reason fails. All these words, Brahman, Nirvana, Allah, Yahweh, Christ, are meaningless to those who cannot get beyond their reason and allow the divine Mystery to shine through its symbol. This is done by faith. Faith is the opening of the mind to the transcendent Reality, the awakening to the eternal Truth.

Christianity has its evolution no less than every other religion. It begins as a sect of Judaism, speaking Aramaic and enclosed in the thought-forms of the Semitic world. Then it breaks out into the Graeco-Roman world and begins to speak the language and to adopt the thought-forms of the Greeks. This process begins at its very inception. The first gospels themselves are translations into Greek of the original Aramaic, interpreting the original message in the light of a new situation, yet always remaining faithful to the original mystery. It is this 'mystery of Christ' which lies at the heart of the gospels and of all the evolution of Christianity. It cannot properly be expressed. The language of the New

Testament is the earliest form of its expression which we possess and comes closest to the original, but the Truth is ever beyond what the words can express. It is the Word of God, the eternal Truth made manifest, the mystery of salvation, of man's encounter with God. It is the mystery which was 'hidden for ages in God'.[1] This is the object of faith, expressed in words but always going beyond words, speaking to the heart, awakening the depths of the soul, bringing illumination, peace, joy. And this Mystery when known in its ultimate ground is one with the mystery of Brahman, Nirvana, Tao, Yahweh, Allah. It is the one Truth, the one Word, the eternal Saccidananda.

The goal of each religion is the same. It is the absolute, transcendent state, the one Reality, the eternal Truth, which cannot be expressed, cannot be conceived. This is the goal not only of all religion, but of all human existence – whether they like it or not, all men are continually attracted by this transcendent Truth. The intellect, in and beyond every formulation by which it seeks to express its thought, is in search of the Absolute. It is made for Being itself, for Truth, for Reality, and it cannot rest satisfied in any partial truth, in any construction of the human mind. It is always being carried beyond itself to the ultimate Truth. The will also is always moved by love of the Infinite. In every human love there is a reaching out towards the Infinite, a desire to transcend itself, to make the total surrender of self. This tendency is present in the atheist and the agnostic, in the ignorant and foolish as well as the wise. It is what gives an infinite value to the human person. Every attempt to deny this tendency, to confine human life to the finite and the temporal, is doomed to failure, because it is fighting against nature. It breaks out of all careful formulations and limited objectives. Perhaps Wittgenstein is the best evidence of this, but Marxism also bears witness to it. It is the redeeming element in all philosophy, which prevents it from ever settling down to a partial vision of the Truth.

This of course is the grace of poetry. The poet, the painter, the artist, is always in touch with this transcendent Mystery – in so far as he is an authentic poet – however much he may be enclosed in the world of the senses and the imagination. He may write of nature or war or human love and passion; he may paint a landscape or a portrait without any 'sacred' character: but it is the presence of the sacred Mystery in his work which makes it poetry. Raïssa Maritain has written well of this when she says that poetry is conceived in 'those depths of the soul where intelligence and desire, intuition and sensibility, imagination and love, have their common source'. Poetry and mysticism both derive from a common source, the ground or depth of the soul, where the Mystery of Being is experienced. But the poet is always driven to 'symbolize' his experience, to express it in words or in paint or in music. The mystic seeks the experience in itself, beyond words or sounds or images.

ELEVEN

Myth and Reality

All religion derives from a mystical experience, transcending thought, and seeks to express this experience, to give it form, in language, ritual, and social organization. Myth is the language of primitive religion: it is the poetic expression of a mystical experience. Myths can only be understood as poetry. They spring from the depths where man encounters the ultimate Mystery of existence and interprets it in poetic form. Prometheus chained to his rock because he stole fire from heaven, Demeter, the Earth Mother, going down into the underworld in search of Persephone, the vegetation god dying and rising again – these are all symbols of the mystery of life. Hinduism still lives in this world of myth. The Hindu gods are all mythological figures, symbols of the divine Mystery, infinitely suggestive but baffling the reason. There is no division between fact and fancy, between the human and the divine, between good and evil. Krishna, for instance, seems to have some basis in history, to have been a man, and he is represented as coming to restore righteousness (*dharma*) on earth. But history is lost in legend, the human is swallowed up in the divine. What is more, he is morally ambivalent. He is a symbol of the highest divinity, yet as a man he is shown to be a trickster, a deceiver, who brings disaster on his people and is finally ignominiously slain. He is a symbol of the purest love but this is expressed in terms of gross sexuality. It is the same with Siva. He is the God of love, of infinite beauty and grace, whose nature is being, knowledge and bliss, the Father, the Saviour, the Friend. Yet his symbol is the lingam and like Krishna he has many wives.

What is the explanation of this? It must be that these figures arise from the undifferentiated ground of the unconscious. They belong to a world of primeval innocence before reason and conscience have been fully developed. In the course of time they were purified by deep philosophic thought and became symbols of the purest mystical experience, but they have never lost their connection with the unconscious, with the world of myth. They have never been properly demythologized. The religion of Israel also arose from this mythical background. The Elohim (who are plural originally, not singular) are clearly mythical beings – they are the 'gods' – Yahweh himself is a mythical figure, who still retains something of his original moral ambivalence, but both these figures have been consistently demythologized and made the subject of a constant moral purification. In the same way there are mythical elements in Israel's history, in the story of Exodus and even later in the concept of the Messiah and his kingdom, but history steadily gains over mythology and the division between fact and fancy, man and God, good and evil, is established. In the New Testament this process is complete. The myth of the god who dies and rises again, of the descent into the underworld, of the man who suffers for bringing fire from heaven, is revealed as history. It takes place at a definite point in space and time, 'under Pontius Pilate', and yet it has all the 'mystery' of the ancient myths. The man Jesus is a human being as real as Socrates and Confucius, yet the divine Mystery is present in his very humanity, making him one with God. Above all, all moral ambivalence has been removed.

Jesus reveals man in the moral perfection for which he was created and at the same time he reveals God as the perfection of love, without the lusts of Krishna or Siva, or the violence and wrath of Yahweh.

In Jesus myth and history meet. Myth reveals the ultimate meaning and significance of life, but it has no hold on history and loses itself in the world of imagination. History of itself, as a mere succession of events, has no meaning. It is the record of events which reveal their meaning only by the significance which the historian finds in them. When historical events are seen to reveal the ultimate significance of life, then myth and history meet. Such are the virgin birth, the resurrection and the ascension. They are historical events, whose records date back to contemporary sources – unlike, for instance, the records of the life of the Buddha, which are so late that fact and fiction can no longer be separated. Yet these events are wholly mythical – they are symbols of ultimate Reality, of the eternal Mystery manifest in space and time, of the new birth by which man becomes God, of the deliverance from sin and death and the achievement of immortality, of man's ascent to the divine, of the return to the One. At this point, history – the world of sensible and psychological appearances – becomes wholly meaningful. Nature reveals the meaning and purpose of her existence, which had been hidden from the beginning of time. Man discovers his real nature and knows himself as a son of God. The divine and the human meet 'without separation and without confusion'.

There is no need to 'demythologize' the New Testament, or the Old Testament for that matter. On the contrary, it is precisely the mythical element that reveals the universal significance of the events. Of themselves the events recorded in the Old and the New Testaments would have a very limited importance; it is the myth that relates them to the eternal drama of man's salvation. Paradise and the Fall, the Exodus and the Promised Land, the Messiah and his kingdom, Jerusalem, the City of God, the new heaven and the new earth – these are the great 'myths' which transform the history of a small people in the Middle East into a symbol of the destiny of man. In the same way, it is the virgin birth, the sacrificial death, the resurrection and the ascension which transform the life of Christ from that of a local prophet and reformer into a symbol of the divine Mystery, a revelation of the plan of God for man's salvation. If it were myth alone, it would be no more than other myths of virgin birth, death and resurrection and ascension to heaven, which are found all over the world. It would be a reflection in the human psyche of the divine Mystery; it would be deeply significant, but it would be poetry, not fact. It would not be an event that has transformed the world. But if it were only an event, if it were simply a case of parthenogenesis, of a man appearing alive after his death, of a body being levitated and disappearing from sight – these would be remarkable phenomena, but they would have a very limited interest. It is the combination of myth and history, of meaning and event, that makes them a revelation of the ultimate meaning and purpose of life.

This seems to have been unique in Israel. Other peoples, like the Hindus, had an immensely rich mythology and drew from it a profound philosophy of life. Others, like the Greeks, had a sense of history, but it was unrelated to their mythology. It was in Israel alone that while the sense of history developed, mythology was seen to be embodied in history. The Promised

Land was the land of Canaan, to which the Israelites were passionately attached – and remain so to this day – but it was also a symbol of the 'heavenly country', the land of heart's desire. The Messiah was to be king of Israel, yet he was also to appear in the clouds of heaven and to rule over all nations. The maiden was to be with child, but she was to be the Virgin of Israel, who was betrothed to God. Again, Jesus saw himself as the suffering servant of Isaiah, who was to bear the sins of the people, but he had to be crucified in brute reality 'under Pontius Pilate'. Even the resurrection was deliberately given a mythical character. 'As Jonah was three days and three nights in the belly of the whale, so will the Son of man be three days and three nights in the heart of the earth.'[1] Yet the events of the resurrection were seen as historical events. The disciples were convinced that they had seen and talked with Jesus after his death.

There is no doubt that the writers of the New Testament believed that the events of the virgin birth and the resurrection had actually taken place. Their stories are quite different from those of the lives of the Buddha, or of the Puranas, or of the apocryphal gospels, where there is no control of history. The stories are from different milieus, put down with simple sincerity, without any concern for harmonization. Of course they were fully aware of their 'mythical' character; they wrote as theologians, but they were no less concerned with the historic events. They were writing a theology of history, and if the history were not true the theology would be invalid. The reason why the truth of these events is doubted by many people in the West today is that the Western mind is prejudiced against myth. It is the defect of the scientific mind. The whole bent of science is to withdraw everything from the sphere of myth, to create a sphere of 'fact' which can be observed and verified. This has its own value and is a necessary discipline of the mind. But it empties life of all meaning. 'Facts' are simply sense-appearances, examined and verified by reason, and such knowledge is necessary to check the mythical faculty. But the world of sense-appearances is, after all, a very limited aspect of human experience. As the Upanishad says: 'Beyond the senses is the mind [the *manas*, the reason], above the mind is the intellect [the *buddhi*, the pure intelligence], above the intellect is the Great Self [the *mahat*, the cosmic consciousness], above the Great Self is the Unmanifest [the world of ideas, the Nous], above the Unmanifest is the Person [*Purusha*], the all-pervading and imperceptible. Beyond the Person, there is nothing.'[2] It is myth that opens the mind to these higher states of consciousness, while the scientist remains shut up in his little world of 'facts'.

TWELVE

The Buddha, Krishna and Christ

What is the difference between the Buddha, Krishna and Christ? All three are 'symbols' of God, that is, of the divine mystery in human terms, but each has his own distinctive character and belongs to a different world of symbols. While Krishna is primarily a legendary character belonging to the world of myth (with all the deep meaning which that word implies), Buddha comes before us as an historical person. Though legends have grown up around him and it is impossible to reconstruct his life as a whole, yet the historical basis remains and a moral character emerges as decisive as that of Jesus or Socrates. He reveals a type of moral perfection and a compassion which is as real and universal as the love of Christ. But still there are differences. The Buddha is the 'enlightened one', who has known the truth and has come to reveal it to the world, but he is not 'God', since Buddhism does not recognize a 'God'. He is said to be *atideva*, 'above the gods', and he is called omniscient. He stands for the ultimate principle of being. He has his *dharmakaya*, his 'body of reality', of absolute being, as well as his *sambhogyakaya*, his 'body of bliss, or spiritual body', and his *nirmanakaya*, his 'body of incarnation'. This brings him very close to Christ, but Buddhism will not allow a personal God. True to its basic intuition, the ultimate reality is conceived in negative terms – it is *sunya*, 'void'. The Buddha himself disappears in this void. This affects also the compassion of the Buddha. His compassion arises from the fact that he sees that all men are deceived and do not know the saving truth of Nirvana. When the truth is known, no compassion remains, since no person remains. Buddhist compassion, therefore, with all its unique beauty, is not the same as Christian love.

What of Krishna, how does he compare with Christ? Though there may have been a historical Krishna – in fact, there were probably two or three – he has become a 'mythical' person, that is a person in whom the symbolic character overshadows the historical. If Krishna had never existed, it would make no real difference. He is for ever a symbol of love incarnate. Through him the Supreme Being – the eternal Saccidananda – reveals himself as love, asking for love in return. 'Give me thy mind and give me thy heart and thy sacrifice and thy adoration. This is my word of promise: thou shalt in truth come to me, for thou art dear to me.'[1] This is a genuine revelation of divine love which has inspired love and worship among Hindus ever since. If we compare this with the love of God revealed in Christ, we must not under-estimate its appeal, but we must note the differences. The love of Krishna is an ideal love; it is manifested in Brindavan, the heavenly city of a mythical world. It is an ecstatic love, a love which draws the 'Gopis' – that is, human souls – out of themselves, to give themselves in ecstatic self-surrender. Above all, it is a joyous love. It is said that Krishna came on earth to enjoy himself – he manifests the *lila*, the 'play' of God, the *ananda*, the 'bliss' of love.

The contrast with the love of Christ could not be more striking. The love of God was revealed in Christ not in poetry but in history. It was shown not in ecstasy but in self-giving for others, in the surrender of his life on the cross. 'The Son of Man came not to be served, but to

serve and to give his life as a ransom for many.'[2] Finally,
it was shown not in play but in an agony of blood and
sweat, not in joy but in suffering. Yet each of these is a
genuine revelation. We cannot afford to neglect either of
them. Christianity also has a place for an ideal love,
which is joyous and ecstatic. The Song of Songs ever
since the time of Origen has found a place in Christian
tradition as a symbol of the love of God for the soul, and
the greatest Christian mystics, St Bernard, Ruysbroeck
and St John of the Cross, speak of the love of God
culminating in a joyous ecstasy. Has Hinduism a place
for a God who suffers and dies on the cross, for a God
who enters into history, for a love which is experienced
in the midst of suffering and dereliction? That perhaps
is the crucial question.

Can one say that Krishna is God? It depends what
exactly one means. That Krishna is the Supreme Being,
the Father of the universe, that he pervades the whole
creation and dwells in the heart of every man, this is
clearly revealed in the Bhagavad Gita. He is 'the
Supreme Brahman, the supreme abode, the supreme
purity, the eternal divine Person, the primeval God, the
unborn, omnipresent Lord.'[3] It would be difficult to deny
the name of God to such a being. Yet again we must
remember that Krishna belongs to the world of myth,
that is, to the archetypal world beyond time and history.
He cannot be judged by ordinary moral standards. When
Krishna was sporting with the Gopis, drawing them
away from their husbands to dance with him, he was
only a boy of thirteen. He does not belong to this world
or to human history. By contrast Jesus does belong to the
world of history. He was 'crucified under Pontius Pilate'.
He also belongs to a mythical world, the world of the
archetypal symbols of Virgin Birth, death and resur-

rection, ascension and glorification. But in him the myth has been located in history. Whereas Hinduism belongs to the Cosmic revelation, the revelation of God in the cosmos and the human soul, Jesus belongs to the historical revelation, the revelation of God in the history of one particular people. What distinguishes this revelation is that it takes place not in the cyclic time of mythology but in historic time. The *avatara* – the 'descent' of God – in Hinduism is a recurrent event; every age in principle has its *avatara*. But in Israel history was seen to have an 'end' – an eschaton – and Jesus was believed to have come at the 'end' of history. It was his plan in the 'fullness of time' – or as Mgr Knox translated it, 'to give history its fulfilment' – to bring all things to a head in Christ.'[4]

Thus each revelation has its own perspective, each has its own unique insight into the eternal mystery, and has to be judged in its own historical context and in its own particular mode of thought. To say that God is a Person is not necessarily to deny that he is impersonal. It is to affirm that the values of personal being, as we know them, in particular the values of knowledge and love and therefore of moral responsibility, exist in the Godhead, but they exist in God in a manner beyond our comprehension, to which our concepts are always inadequate, and therefore to say that God is impersonal can also be true. It signifies that the Godhead – or whatever name we give to the ultimate mystery of being – is so far beyond any concept which we can form of a person, that it is better not to use the word. And in fact, we often find that the Christian concept of God sometimes becomes so personal that it needs to be corrected by the impersonalism of Buddhism. Again to say that God is moral perfection signifies that all that we can conceive of moral perfection, of goodness, kindness, gentleness, mercy, pity, grace and love exists in the Godhead, but again in a way beyond our conception. To insist too much on the moral character of God can narrow our conception and lose something of the ecstasy of joy which is found in Krishna. Each revelation is therefore complementary to the other and indeed, in each religion we find a tendency to stress first one aspect of the Godhead and then another, always seeking the equilibrium in which the ultimate truth will be found.

THIRTEEN

Death and Resurrection

We must never forget the 'terrible' aspect of God. If God is represented as love, it is easy to form a sentimental idea of the Godhead which bears no relation to reality. It is this sentimental conception of God which many people rightly reject, calling themselves atheists. If God is all mercy and love, why does he permit so much suffering in the world? How to explain the concentration camps of Hitler and Stalin, the destruction of Hiroshima and Nagasaki? Every serious religious tradition admits this 'terrible' aspect of the Godhead. In the Upanishad it is said, 'This Brahman is like a drawn sword',[1] and Krishna in the Gita is revealed as 'all-devouring Time'.[2] In Buddhism the supreme Truth is compared to the thunderbolt. In the Epistle to the Hebrews it is said, 'Our God is a consuming fire.'[3] But it is in Judaism and Islam that this aspect is most evident. Yahweh is above all a 'terrible' God – 'mighty and terrible are his deeds'[4] – and Islam strikes one at first as a religion of fear. Yet Yahweh is also a God 'merciful and gracious, slow to anger, and abounding in steadfast love and faithfulness',[5] and Allah is before all the 'merciful, the compassionate'. The same paradox is present in Christ. He can say, 'Come to me, all who labour and are heavy-laden, and I will give you rest. Take my yoke upon you, and learn from me; for I am gentle and lowly in heart.'[6] But he can also say, 'Depart from me, you cursed, into the eternal fire prepared for the devil and his angels.'[7] The modern world finds it difficult to believe in hell, but it finds it equally difficult to believe in heaven. We would like to have a comfortable mediocrity, not a love which demands all or nothing. The terror and the mystery are both present in the crucifixion and this remains the only 'answer' to the problem that can be found. The cross is the supreme symbol of the mystery, the point at which the eternal truth finally breaks through the veil.

What then is the meaning of the cross? It is the point of convergence of two opposite movements. On the one hand, there is the movement of man's ascent to God, the movement to transcend the barriers of space and time, to reach towards the infinite Transcendence. This is the movement of oriental thought, the ascent to the Brahman, to Nirvana, to the Tao, the passing beyond the boundaries of human thought, the death of the ego and the awakening to the divine. When Jesus surrendered his life on the cross, he brought to fulfilment this movement of the human soul; he accomplished the total surrender of man to God, of the human to the divine; he achieved the final death of the self to this world and raised it to eternal life in the resurrection. This is the one movement which was accomplished on the cross. The other movement is the descent of the divine into this world, the movement of incarnation. From the beginning of creation the Spirit has been communicating itself to matter. Every stage of evolution, from matter to life to mind, is a communication of the Spirit, an incarnation of God. Every religion reflects this movement of divine descent, God making himself known to man, the Spirit communicating itself in love. This is the movement especially of Judaism and Islam, the infinite, holy, transcendent One, making himself known, communicating his Spirit. On the cross this movement of divine descent met the corresponding movement of man's ascent to God, the movement of God's self-giving in love to man and the movement of man's self-giving in love to God met in one person and the salvation of the world was accomplished.

But this was accomplished at the extreme limit of human suffering, at the point where all the powers of hell were concentrated. Heaven and hell met at this point – the total transcendence, the final fulfilment, the utmost joy, and on the other hand, the powers of darkness, the forces of disintegration and death, the utmost loneliness: 'My God, my God, why hast thou forsaken me?' This is where the total reality of the human situation is revealed, its exposure to the ultimate Truth. Of course, in a sense these forces of evil are *maya*. They have no ultimate reality. They are negative forces, the negation of Truth, the negation of Love. But they have acquired a terrible reality. Sin has invested them with a fearful power. Sin is the consent to unreality, the willing acceptance of an illusion, but for those who have succumbed to the illusion, its power is almost irresistible – almost, but not quite. On the cross this illusion was shattered, and for those who accept the cross, who die to the self, the illusion has no more power.

In every religious tradition it has been known that in order to see God – that is, to know the Truth, to encounter the final Reality – one must die. In fact, there is a threefold death through which everyone must pass – a death to the world, a death to the flesh and a death to the ego. These are the three great illusions which bind us to unreality and prevent us from knowing the Truth, and at no time have they been stronger than they are today. The illusion of the world – the world of science and technology, of motor cars and aeroplanes, of radio and television, of telephones and cinema, of computers and space flights, of contraception and atom bombs – all this creates a world of illusion to which one must be utterly dead, if one wants to know the Truth. From beginning to end it is a world of sense-appearances, a system of idolatry, given a greater power than ever before and exercising a fascination which few can resist.

Then there is the illusion of the flesh, the endless fascination of sex, not merely cultivated and exploited by every means that art can devise, but worshipped and deified, made the centre of attraction and regarded as the source of life. This is the second death one must die, death to the flesh, to every movement of passion and desire, not merely to every outward form of expression but to the slightest movement of desire. 'Everyone who looks at a woman lustfully has already committed adultery with her in his heart.'[8] The third death is the death of the ego, and this is the hardest of all. One may resist the fascination of the world and the flesh, but who can resist the love of the self? That personality which everyone is so anxious to cultivate, power, reputation, success, the fame of the scientist, the scholar, the athlete, the film-star, the politician – all this is the illusion of the ego, which binds the soul more securely to unreality than any other power. It pursues the spiritual man also to the very gates of heaven – no one is secure from this illusion except he who has died with Christ and can say, 'The world has been crucified to me, and I to the world'[9] and 'It is no longer I who live, but Christ who lives in me.'[10]

But what happens when we have died to the world, the flesh and the self, when we have seen through the illusion and faced reality? Why then we begin to live to the real world, the real flesh and the real self. This is the paradox which it is so difficult to understand. It is only when you have renounced the world that you can really enjoy the world;[11] it is only when you have renounced the flesh that you can take a pure delight in the flesh; it is only when you have renounced yourself that you can discover your real being. This has been proved over and over again in history. All the great cultures of the world, the Chinese, the Indian, the Islamic and the Christian, were built up on this principle. It is clearest of all in India. Both Buddhist and Hindu cultures are based on a radical renunciation of the world, on a recognition of the illusion of this world and of the need for total transcendence. And it is from this spirit of renunciation that there sprang the miracles of art and architecture, of poetry and music, of philosophy and theology, the growth of political and economic life, the development of craftsmanship and social organization, and, of course, the marvellous flowering of the religious spirit, which have made Indian civilization one of the richest in the world. In China it was the presence of Buddhism and the influence of Taoism, with its cult of poverty, simplicity and humility, of *wuwei*, that is, of active inactivity or action in inaction, which gave to Chinese culture its immeasurable refinement. In Islam it was Sufism, the ascetic and mystical movement whose goal was *fana*, the passing away of the self into the Absolute, which transfigured Islamic civilization and gave it its transcendent beauty. Finally it was the monastic movement in Christendom, the deliberate and total rejection of the world, the flesh and the self, which laid the foundations of the whole medieval civilization. The modern world began with the Reformation and the Renaissance, with the rejection of the monastic ideal and the cult of the world, the flesh and the ego.

Poverty, chastity and obedience – the renunciation of the world, the flesh and the ego – are the basis not only of all religious life but of all human life. Detachment is the universal law. You cannot enjoy anything until you have learned to be detached from it. It is not the drunkard who enjoys wine, or the glutton who enjoys food, or the sensualist who enjoys love. The perfect artist – whether dancer or actor or athlete – is not one who indulges the body but one who has mastered the body. His art becomes a yoga – a means of union, union of the powers of the body in harmony, union of body and soul in harmony, union of body and soul with the inner Spirit. But this is only attained when body and soul are 'sacrificed' to the Spirit. As long as they retain their independence, there can be no yoga, no harmony. This is the death which body and soul have to undergo, the sacrifice of their autonomy, their surrender to the inner Spirit. This was what was lost at the Renaissance. Body and soul were released from their obedience to the inner law of the Spirit and given their autonomy, just as the economic and political orders were gradually released from their obedience to the law of the Spirit and given their autonomy. In the ancient world every human activity was in principle a yoga – a means of union with the divine. Ploughing and sowing, spinning and weaving, carpentry and building, dance and song, poetry and philosophy, even war and government, were all seen as integral activities of the whole man, relating man to the cosmos and to the cosmic law; hence there was a balance and harmony in life, a balance and harmony always threatened by sin but always preserved in principle. But in the modern world the principle of balance and harmony has been lost. This is the real cause of the alienation of man, not, as Marx imagined, the mere conflict between labour and capital, the workers having no control over the means of production. The existence of a 'proletariat' is a sign of a lack of balance in the social order. Because of the industrial revolution work has ceased to be an integrating power in human life, it has become mechanical and 'soul-destroying', and with it the whole balance between man and nature has been disturbed.

Modern science – that is, the science which has developed since the Renaissance – is intrinsically defective both in its principles and in its methods. It is defective in principle because it looks upon the material world as an independent reality, and it is defective in its methods because it treats the material world as though it obeyed mechanical laws which are independent of the law of the Spirit. But in reality the material world is a part – and an inferior part – of a greater whole. According to ancient tradition there are three 'worlds' – the physical, the psychic and the spiritual – and those worlds are interdependent as an integrated whole. Man himself is a miniature world. He has a physical body which obeys the laws of matter but is dependent on the soul with its psychic powers, and this in turn is dependent on the Spirit by which man is related to the Source of being. To treat the body, as modern medicine does, as though it were an independent entity, unrelated to the soul and the Spirit, is against nature. Many doctors today are beginning to discover that disease is psychosomatic and that the body cannot be properly treated apart from the soul. It is only one further step to discover that all disease has a spiritual cause and is ultimately due to sin – to the breach in the harmony between body, soul and Spirit.

This is the root-cause of the 'disease' of modern

civilization. Matter is separated from spirit, body from soul, man from nature. Of course, this conflict has been present in the world from the beginning; it is the effect of original sin. But in every ancient culture the principle of integration was preserved. That is why the materialist and the atheist were always regarded as anti-social and anti-human. They deny the principle on which human society rests. This is not to deny that there are laws of matter which can be studied in isolation – the astonishing success of modern science is evidence of this. But these laws have to be related to the psychic laws on which they depend, and these in turn to the ultimate spiritual law. Goethe was one of the few in modern times who was able to conceive a science of this nature. So he wrote, 'Perhaps there was the possibility of another method, one which would not tackle nature merely by dissecting and particularizing, but show her at work, and alive, manifesting herself in her wholeness, in every single part of her being.'[12] This is a vision of an integral science which has yet to be realized.

What is the reason that modern society has lost this principle of integration? The reason seems to be this. In the Middle Ages – that is, in the years AD 500–1500 – not only in Europe but also in China and India and the Islamic world, a creative synthesis was achieved, in which the physical and psychic and spiritual worlds were marvellously integrated. The economic, social, political and cultural orders were all conceived as a harmonious unity in which each man was related to nature, to his fellow-man and to the divine source of truth and justice, the *dharma*, the eternal Law. Of course, this order was being continually threatened with destruction by the forces of disintegration, but the principle of integration was preserved in the 'perennial philosophy', the traditional wisdom, whether Confucian or Buddhist or Hindu or Islamic or Christian. A Chinese landscape of the Sung dynasty, the Ajanta frescoes, the Hindu temple, the Gothic cathedral, the Taj Mahal, are all alike evidence of this creative synthesis, of the harmony of heaven and earth, of the right order of human life. In this period we can see the model of human perfection, what human life was intended to be. After this period this creative synthesis began to disintegrate. The Reformation and the Renaissance, the 'Enlightenment' and the French Revolution, the Russian and Chinese revolutions, are all stages in this process of disintegration. Now, after nearly five hundred years, the process seems to be almost complete, and there are those who question whether our present civilization can survive for more than fifty years.

Protestantism broke up the organic unity of the mystical Body of Christ, that divine-human order which the Church had established in the West, and made each man an isolated individual. Rationalism set the human mind free from the divine and enclosed each man in the limits of his own reason. Finally, communism came to deprive man of his basic liberty and enslave him to the material world, separated from the divine and dominated by human reason. But this is only one side of the picture. On the other side the religious traditions had each lost their creative power. Catholicism in Western Europe, Orthodoxy in Russia, Confucianism in China, like Hinduism in India and Islam throughout the Middle East, had all alike declined and become closed in on themselves, so that the divine Truth, which was in each one of them, could not exert its power. At the same time each of these revolutionary movements had released immense forces – humanism and democracy, science and technology, capitalism and socialism – which could no longer be controlled by any religious order.

Of course, all these movements have positive values, but they have been vitiated by a violent break with the *sanatana dharma*, the divine order, by which human life must be ruled. The principles of all these movements are to be·found in the perennial philosophy on which all ancient civilization was based, and it would have been possible for the modern world to have developed organically from the ancient world instead of making a violent break with tradition. Protestantism could have been a movement of reform within Catholicism, bringing about that renewal of the Church by a return to the Bible for which we are looking today. Humanism and democracy, science and technology, capitalism and socialism, could all have grown out of the medieval order of Europe and India and China, in which they were already present in principle. But each has advanced by a violent break with the ancient order and thrown the whole world out of balance. The only way in which the world can recover is by a return to the eternal religion, the divine law on which human society is based. But this eternal religion cannot be discovered now exclusively in any one religion. We cannot return to the past forms of Catholicism or Buddhism or Confucianism or Hindu or Islamic orthodoxy. Each religion has to return to its source in the eternal religion, freeing itself from the limitations which historical circumstances have imposed upon it and rediscovering the principles on which modern society must be based.

FOURTEEN

The Eternal Religion

Where, then, is this eternal religion – the *sanatana dharma*, as the Hindus call it – to be found? It is to be found in every religion as its ground or source, but it is beyond all formulation. It is the reality behind all rites, the truth behind all dogmas, the justice behind all laws. But it is also to be found in the heart of every man. It is the law 'written on their hearts'.[1] It is not known by sense or reason but by the experience of the soul in its depths. Of this it has been said: 'Thy natural senses cannot possess God or unite thee to him; nay, thy inward faculties of understanding, will, and memory, can only reach after God, but cannot be the place of his habitation in thee. But there is a root or depth in thee from whence all these faculties come forth, as lines from a centre or as branches from the body of the tree. This depth is called the Centre, the *Fund* or Bottom of the soul. This depth is the unity, the eternity, I had almost said the infinity of thy soul; for it is so infinite that nothing can satisfy it or give it any rest but the infinity of God.'[2] It is in this depth that all true religion is to be found. It is the source from which all religion springs, the goal to which it aspires, and it is present in the heart of every man. It was from this Centre that man fell and it is to this Centre that he must return. Every religion seeks to make this known and to map out the path of return.

Each man must therefore discover this Centre in himself, this Ground of his being, this Law of his life. It is hidden in the depths of every soul, waiting to be discovered. It is the treasure hidden in a field, the pearl of great price.[3] It is the one thing which is necessary,[4] which can satisfy all our desires and answer all our needs. But it is hidden now under deep layers of habit and convention. The world builds up a great protective barrier round it. It is the original paradise from which we have all come – as Wordsworth said, 'Heaven lies about us in our infancy.' We were all once innocent and pure and holy, as we came from God, but we have fallen into this world, and an angel with a flaming sword prevents our return. All these mysteries are hidden in the unconscious. There still stands the original paradise, there the Fall takes place in each one of us, the trauma of birth into this world. There the layers of habit and convention are formed, binding us to this world, beginning their work while we are yet in the womb, weaving the great web of *maya*, which hides us from our true Self and makes us aliens from our home. But everywhere the path of return is to be found. Every myth and ritual of primitive religion is a revelation of the hidden mysteries of the unconscious and a pathway to the discovery of the Self.

If we would find the path of return we must be willing to learn from every ancient tradition, from African and Asian tribal religion, from that of the Australian aborigines and the American Indian. All these people who have been suppressed and almost eliminated by the white races bear within themselves the treasures of the ancient wisdom. By returning to them we are returning to our own past, to the wisdom of the unconscious which has been suppressed in us, to the heart of the child which is hidden in every man. Our civilization will remain for ever psychologically unbalanced until it has done justice to these people. The Negro will remain a perpetual challenge to white civilization until the wisdom which he possesses, the intuitive wisdom of primeval man, has been recognized. In all these people the sense of man's solidarity with nature has been preserved. Nature is for them not what it is to the scientific mind, an external object to be studied by cold reason, but a living part of his own being. He knows himself as part of nature, as having kinship with the earth and the sky, with the plants and animals and birds. He knows himself in the deep ground of the unconscious as a child in the womb of Mother Nature, where the world, as Thales said, is 'full of gods'. The gods are not fictions of the imagination; they are the living powers of nature, present in earth and sea and sky. They belong to the 'psychic' world, the world which we only know in dream, but which is no less real than the physical world. In this world there are also the spirits of the ancestors. Man knows himself not as isolated in this outer world of time and space, but as in communion with the spirits of the dead. In the depths of the unconscious we are one with all nature and all humanity, open to the divine Spirit which is in all, not enclosed in the prison of a separate individuality in an alien world.

This ancient wisdom is enshrined in a Hindu temple. The temple is the image both of the cosmos and of the soul. To go round a temple visiting the shrines of the different gods is to bring the soul into harmony with the powers of the cosmos and to discover the 'centre' both of the cosmos and the soul. The centre of the temple is the *garbha-griha* – the 'womb' in which the lingam and yoni are to be found, symbols of the marriage of the male and the female which takes place in this depth or centre of the soul. The ritual of the temple is likewise an external sign of the inner transformation of the soul, the discovery of the divine life hidden in the soul. The breaking of the coconut is a symbol of the breaking of the hard outer shell of the soul to discover the pure white substance and the sweet milk of the divine life within. The ashes put on the forehead are a symbol of the burning up of the lower self, the sinful ego, and the manifestation of the true Self from which all impurities have been burnt away. The red spot placed between the eyes is a symbol of the 'third eye', the eye of wisdom which is 'single', as opposed to the two eyes which see the world of duality. Thus everything is intended to enable the soul to discover its 'Centre', to free it from the separated ego and integrate it in the cosmic unity. It is a concrete symbol of the path of return to the Self, to the knowledge of God.

All these religions derive from the cosmic covenant,[5] the universal revelation given to all mankind. It is a revelation of God through nature and the soul. The whole cosmos is a revelation of God. To an unsophisticated mind the order and beauty of the universe is a revelation of the wisdom and goodness of the Creator. The sky stretching immeasurably above him is a sign of his transcendence, its boundless space of his infinity, its abiding for ever unchanged, while all things beneath it change, of his eternity.[6] The sky embraces the whole world and all the worlds of the gods above, therefore it is a symbol of the Supreme Being. Its gaze penetrates everywhere, therefore it is all-knowing. It sends down the warm rays of the sun and the rain from the clouds to nourish the earth, therefore it is benevolent. But it is also the sphere of thunder and lightning, therefore it is to be feared. Fear and terror, awe and wonder, worship and adoration, hope and expectation, praise and thanksgiving are all evoked by the sky. The Chinese call it *tien*, 'heaven', and for them it is the symbol of the Godhead and the 'way of heaven' is the universal law. The ancient Indians spoke of Dyaus-pita, the Sky-Father, the Greeks called him Zeus Pater, the Latins Jupiter. The most primitive tribes in all parts of the world pray to the Sky-Father, and when Jesus taught his disciples to pray, he could find no other words to address God but 'Father in heaven'. Such is the continuity of religion.

For modern man, of course, all this is meaningless. The sky, like the earth, has been profaned. It is merely a space through which he travels for his business or pleasure. The moon is no longer a divine power influencing the life of man, but mere matter of which specimens may be taken for chemical analysis. There are no gods in outer space. And yet how true is this 'scientific' view of the universe? It is the universe seen from one point of view in its measurable, quantitative aspect, just as the human body can be observed simply as a biological specimen and medicine can treat it very effectively in that way. But is a man only the body which is laid out on the operating table? Has he not a mind and a will, thoughts and feelings, hopes and desires? How do we know that the stars are not 'intelligences', as Aristotle and the Arabian philosophers believed? How do we know that there are not gods or angels in outer space? What, after all, is outer space? Both space and time are categories of the mind: there is no time or space without a mind to measure them. As the Upanishad says, 'There is a space within the heart in which all space is contained. Both heaven and earth are contained within it, both fire and air, both sun and moon, both lightning and stars. Everything that exists is contained in that "City of Brahman", all beings and all desires.'[7] When we pass beyond the mind, with its measuring faculties, its categories of time and space, we discover the true Self, the Ground of the universe, the City of Brahman, in which all is contained. And there, all things are not dead matter but life and intelligence. There all things are found as they exist eternally in the Word, of which it is said, 'That which has been made was life in him.'[8]

The gods are not to be known by the senses or by scientific instruments or by mathematical calculations. No amount of exploration of outer space will discover them. They are hidden within, beyond the mind, beyond the senses. As the *Katha* Upanishad says: 'The self-existent pierced the opening of the senses so that they turn outwards: therefore man looks outwards not inwards into himself. But one wise man, desiring immortality, looked inwards and saw the Self.'[9] This is the revolution which has to take place in the mind of Western man. He has been turning outwards to the world of the senses for centuries and losing himself in outer space. He has to learn again to turn inwards and find his Self. He has to learn to explore not outer space but the inner space within the heart, to make that long and difficult journey to the Centre, to the inner depth and height of being, which Dante described in *The Divine Comedy*, compared with which the exploration of the moon and the other planets is the play of children.

But how to find the path to the Centre, the way of return? Again the Upanishad answers: 'That Self cannot be attained by the study of the scriptures, nor by the intellect nor by much learning. He whom the Self chooses, by him the Self can be attained.'[10] The Self, the Truth, the inner Centre of being, is not to be reached by any human effort, not by science, not by philosophy, not by theology, nor by any technique, still less by any technology or social engineering. It is not within the grasp of the mind. It is not the mind which grasps the

Self, it is the Self which grasps the mind. It is the mind itself which must capitulate, the rational, scientific mind, which wants to dominate the world. As the Upanishad again says: 'The wise should surrender speech in mind, mind in the knowing Self, the knowing Self in the great Self, the great Self in the Self of peace.'[11] This is the path of wisdom, the path of return to the Self. Speech, by which the mind goes out of itself and communicates with the external world, has to be surrendered to the mind, the mind to the knowing Self, the true Self, the inner person, who knows not by reflection on the senses but by its own inherent powers. Then this inner, individual Self must be surrendered to the great Self, the universal, cosmic consciousness, of which each individual is a reflection, and this cosmic consciousness to the Self of peace, the peace which passes understanding, the One beyond thought, who reveals himself only to those who are totally surrendered to him.

It must not be thought that when reason surrenders to the Self it loses any of its powers. On the contrary, it is only then that it rises to the height of its power. The mind of a Sankara or an Aquinas is equal to that of any modern scientist or philosopher, but it draws on sources of wisdom which raise it to a higher power and carry it beyond their reach. Bertrand Russell was a baby compared with Sankara or Aquinas. His mind, in spite of its excellence, could never get beyond the world of the senses and its extension in logic and mathematics. But Sankara and Aquinas, though no less logical and rational, were both mystics who had experienced the reality of a world which transcends the senses and could bring their intelligence to bear on that. Indeed the trouble with both of them has been that they built up a system which was so logically perfect that it has obscured their mystical vision. Their followers have accepted the system and ignored the vision. The *advaitic* vision of Sankara was a unique insight into the eternal Truth, but his philosophical system when this is ignored is open to grave objections. Aquinas at the end of his life declared that all that he had written seemed to him like straw in comparison with what he had seen, but his followers erected his theological system deprived of its mystic vision into a rigid framework of dogma to be imposed on the human mind. Al-Ghazali[12] did for the mystical vision of Islam what Sankara and Aquinas did for that of Hinduism and Christianity, and what Nagarjuna[13] and Vasubandhu,[14] the doctors of the Mahayana, did for Buddhism. They gave a rational and logical form to the mystical insight into the transcendent Truth.

But in all these systems the danger is that the logical structure and rational doctrine will obscure the mystical vision, so inherent is the tendency of the rational mind to seek to dominate the truth which it should serve. This is the danger of all religion. It begins with a mystical experience, the experience of the seers of the Upanishads, of the Buddha under the Bo tree, of the Hebrew prophets and the apostles at Pentecost, of Mahomet receiving the message of the Koran. But this experience has to be put into words; it has to descend into the outer world and take the forms of human speech. Already at this stage it is open to misinterpretation; the conflict between the letter and the spirit begins. Then the logical and rational mind comes and creates systems of thought: heresies and sects spring up, and the one Truth is divided. This is due to the defect of the rational mind, imposing its narrow concepts and categories on the universal truth. Yet it cannot be avoided, because the Truth must be proclaimed; it has to be communicated and this cannot be done without words, which both express and veil the Truth. All sacred scriptures, the Vedas, the Buddhist Sutras, the Bible, the Koran, are subject to this law. They betray the Truth which they proclaim.

In each religion it is necessary to go back beyond its formulations, whether in scripture or tradition, to the original inspiration. All scriptures and traditions are historically conditioned; they belong to a particular age and culture and are expressed in a particular language and mode of thought. But behind these historic forms of expression lies the original Mystery, the revealed Truth. To discover this Mystery, to enter into this Truth, it is necessary to participate in the original revelation. No amount of profane scholarship will discover the truth of the Bible, the Vedas or the Koran. One must receive the Spirit by which the scriptures were inspired; one must be initiated into the Truth. This is why in ancient times only Brahmins were allowed to study the Vedas; they alone were held to possess the secret of their interpretation. In the same way, the Catholic Church claimed to have authority to interpret the Bible, because the Spirit by which the Bible was inspired dwelt in her. Protestantism opened the Bible to the private interpretation of every man, and now every Tom, Dick and Harry is free to interpret it for himself. But the Bible, like other scriptures, will only open its meaning to those who have received the gift of the Spirit and are initiated into the Truth. But it is not possible to confine the Spirit to one scripture alone. We have to learn to recognize the voice of the Spirit in every scripture and discover the hidden Source from which all scriptures come.

This hidden Source can only be found by those who follow the path of the traditional wisdom. In every religion there is a tradition of faith, in which the truth of the revelation is preserved. The formulation of this tradition is subject to continuous development and may give rise to many different sects and schools, but one can always find the mystery of faith behind its formulations. Saivism, Vaishnavism and Shaktism, and the different schools of Vedanta in Hinduism; Hinayana and Mahayana Buddhism, with their different schools; the Sunni and the Shia sects in Islam, and their different schools of philosophy; Catholicism, Orthodoxy and Protestantism within Christianity, with their different theologies, all are different expressions of the one Truth of revelation, each with its particular insight. But one must learn to discern among these conflicting and partial views the principle which unites them, which transcends their differences and reconciles their conflicts. This Truth is to be found beyond all the formulations of the schools and beyond all the revelations of the scriptures, in the inner depths of the heart, beyond words and thoughts, where the divine Word is spoken and the mystery of Being is made known.

What is this essential Truth of all religion, in the light of which every scripture has to be understood? Of course, it cannot properly be put into words, yet there are words and phrases which symbolize it, which point towards it for those who have eyes to see. Jesus spoke of it as the 'kingdom of God' or the 'kingdom of heaven'. This was the essential content of his message: 'The kingdom of God is at hand.'[15] But what is this kingdom of God? Let us say that it means the divine life among men. This is the essential message of all religion. The infinite, transcendent, holy Mystery, which is what is signified by 'God' or 'Heaven', is present in the world, has its kingdom, its reign, its dwelling among men. Is not this the message of all the scriptures? 'This Brahman, this Self, smaller than the small, greater than the great, is hidden in the heart of every creature.'[16] 'The sun radiates its splendour on all alike: in like manner do the Tathagatas [Buddhas] radiate the truth of noble Wisdom without recourse to words and on all alike.'[17] 'I will walk among you, and will be your God, and you shall be my people',[18] says Yahweh. 'I am closer to you than your jugular vein',[19] says the Koran. Yet these are only words which point to the Truth. We cannot properly say what 'God' is, what is this Brahman, what is this Truth, this noble Wisdom, what is the kingdom of heaven. We have to meditate on these words in the heart, until the Truth shines out and enlightens us, until we experience the presence of God, the kingdom of heaven, within.

All external religion, with its rites and dogmas and organization, exists for no other reason but to lead men to the knowledge – which is also the experience – of this inner mystery. The Church exists for the sake of the kingdom of God. This kingdom is universal, it is the presence of God among men. It has existed from the beginning, in all times and in all places. Every religion bears witness to it: each represents it according to its own particular mode of thought and experience. Each religion has its own particular insight and its own particular limitations. We have to learn to detect the insight and to recognize the limitations. The limitations come from time and place and circumstance, from economic, social and political conditions; the insight comes from the eternal Wisdom reflected in them. The eternal Truth has to be expressed in the forms of space and time, under social and historical conditions, yet these very forms will always tend to betray it. This was the basis of St Paul's attitude to the law. The Law of Moses was given by God. It was the expression of eternal Wisdom in the economic and social and political conditions of a particular people in a particular period of history. As such it was a divine revelation; it established that people in a unique relation with God, that is, with the eternal Ground of being. But the historical conditions, social and political and religious, of Israel were continually changing, like those of every other people, and by the time of Christ the Law of Moses was no longer an adequate expression of the divine Truth. Its doctrine, its ritual and its social organization had all to be transformed in accordance with the very principles which had given them birth. It was the tragedy of Israel that it refused to grow with history, to allow itself to be transfigured according to the divine plan.

The Church today is in the same position as Israel in the time of Christ. The Church was founded by Christ. He gave it the basis of an organization – Peter and the other apostles; a ritual – baptism and eucharist; and a doctrine – concerning the kingdom of God. This Church was intended to be the nucleus of a people, in whom God was to be present by his Spirit, leading them into all truth. In the course of time this Church inevitably developed according to the historical conditions in which it was placed. It left its Jewish matrix and grew up in the Graeco-Roman world, developing its theology through contact with Greek philosophy, its organization according to the pattern of the Roman Empire, and its ritual according to the customs of the time. Finally, in the Middle Ages, it achieved a perfect synthesis of organization, ritual and doctrine which embodied the divine truth committed to it in a concrete historical form. This synthesis, as Newman was to show, was a genuine development of the original apostolic tradition. In medieval Christendom the eternal wisdom was manifested in a marvellous creative synthesis, economic, social, political, cultural, philosophical and theological; in every sphere the human soul rose to the summit of its capacity within the limits of its historical situation, reaching to the height and the depth of mystical experience. But this synthesis was historically conditioned; at the very moment of its consummate achievement the seeds of disintegration were already present in it. The Renaissance itself began in the Middle Ages. New languages, new nations, new economic and social conditions and patterns of thought were emerging, and the medieval Church was unable to adapt itself to this changing world. Like Judaism after the return from captivity, it closed in on itself. It preserved its structure of organization and ritual and doctrine unchanged, but lost its capacity for creative growth.

This is the challenge to the Church today. The structure of doctrine and ritual and organization which it has inherited are no longer adequate to express the divine Mystery, like those of Israel in the time of Christ. The very principle of divine life which originally created those structures is pressing for their transformation. For the eternal Wisdom which remains ever the same has to be manifested in the ever-changing forms of history and society, of language, thought, culture and social organization. The Church has a basic structure which derives from the New Testament, alike of doctrine, of ritual and of organization, but the historical development of this structure is subject to continual change. It is the Graeco-Roman structure which was built on the original Jewish basis that is now breaking down. There is nothing in this, whether it is its dogmatic formulas, or its sacramental system or its hierarchical organization, which is not subject to change. We have to recover the original inspiration which created the Church from the ruins of Judaism. The struggle between the letter and the spirit, the law and grace, has to be renewed, as it has continually in all religion. There is nothing which remains unchallenged, no doctrine, no discipline, no law, no custom. What is demanded, as was demanded of Israel, is nothing less than a death and resurrection. ' "Destroy this temple, and in three days I will raise it up" ... But he spoke of the temple of his body.'[20]

It is this Body of Christ which has to undergo this transformation, this temple of the eternal Wisdom. From the beginning of the world this temple has been building – the whole creation is the temple of God. From the beginning of history this Body of Christ, which is the body of humanity, in which the divine Spirit dwells, has been growing, age by age. Every religion has contributed to the building of this temple, every human being is a member of this Body. Christ is the cornerstone of this temple, the head of this Body, which is the 'pleroma', the 'fullness' of him who fills all in all.[21] Now the Church is this Body of Christ. It is the visible structure in which this mystery of the divine life among men is being manifested. But it is not possible to conceive this Church in isolation from the rest of the world. This divine Mystery is present everywhere in the hearts of all men. It is present in every religion. The mystery of the Church, which is the mystery of the divine life among men, has to be seen in the light of this universal revelation. It is not sufficient to return to the Bible to discover the original source of Christianity. The biblical revelation has to be seen in the context of history as a stage in the manifestation of the Word of God, of the eternal Wisdom, which has been present to the world from the beginning.

This same process of critical evaluation has to take

place in each religion. No religion can now remain in isolation. The revelations of the Vedas, of the Buddhist Sutras and of the Koran have to be evaluated in the light of the biblical revelation and of one another. Each has to be seen as a unique revelation of the eternal Truth, the one Word, manifested under particular historical conditions. In each religion the limitations of these historical conditions have to be discerned, and the essential Truth, which is ultimately One, to be discovered. But this essential Truth cannot be put into words. It is not to be discovered by any process of dialectic. It is known in the silence, in the stillness of all the faculties, in the depth of the soul, beyond word and thought. Every religion, by means of its doctrine and ritual and organization, is intended to lead to this transcendent Knowledge, this experience of ultimate Reality, this participation in the divine life. In Hindu terms it is the knowledge of the Self, the divine Saccidananda. In Buddhist terms it is the experience of Nirvana. In Muslim terms it is *fana* and *baqa* – the passing away and the life in God. For the Jew it is the knowledge of Yahweh, for a Christian it is the knowledge of 'the love of Christ which surpasses knowledge'.[22]

FIFTEEN

The Christian Mystery

Every religious doctrine always ends in mystery. According to Christian faith the mystery of the Godhead is revealed as a Trinity. But what is this Trinity? It has been put into conceptual terms in the formula 'three persons in one nature or essence'. But 'persons', 'nature' and 'essence' are simply terms of Greek philosophy which have been used to make this mystery intelligible to the rational mind. The mystery itself derives from the experience of Jesus. Jesus experienced himself in relation to God as a son to his father,[1] but his sonship was not merely temporal but eternal. He knew himself as coming from the Father not only in time but in eternity.[2] He knew himself as eternally one with the Father, as dwelling in the Father and the Father in him.[3] Again, he knew himself as communicating in the Spirit, which comes from God and is communicated to the world, and this also not only in time but in eternity.[4] To understand the mystery of the Trinity it is necessary to participate in the experience of Jesus. It is necessary to receive the Spirit of God, to share in the divine life and so to become the son of God, to be one with Jesus as he is one with the Father.[5] This is the mystery of Christianity, this participation in the inner life of the Godhead, a mystery which cannot be expressed in words, but which is indicated by analogy by the words 'Father', 'Son' and 'Spirit'. If we stop at the words or the concepts signified by them, we shall always remain outside, unenlightened. But if we pass beyond the words and the concepts to the reality signified by them, then we know the Truth, then we are one with God.

It is the same with the incarnation. Jesus knew himself as a man, a man like us in all things except for sin.[6] He is man as God intended him to be, as every man aspires to be. He is the perfect man, the model of human nature. But he also knew himself in the depths of his being, in the eternal ground of his soul, as God, as the Word of God expressing the mind of God, as the Son manifesting the Father.[7] This mystery has been expressed by saying that in the person of Jesus there are two natures, a divine and a human nature. He is perfect God and perfect man. But again, 'person' and 'nature' are terms of Greek philosophy: they translate the mystery of Christ into rational terms. But if we would know the mystery, we must share in the experience of Jesus. We must know ourselves as sons of God, eternally coming forth from the Father, as words of God expressing his mind. We have to know ourselves as God, God by participation in the divinity of Christ, as we participate in his humanity.

This mystery of the kingdom of God, of the divine life among men, is revealed, then, in the doctrine of the Trinity and the Incarnation, of the Father sending his Son into the world and communicating his Spirit, of the Word becoming flesh, the eternal Wisdom manifesting itself, in a human life. But every religion needs not only a doctrine but also a ritual. The divine Mystery has to be expressed not only in words but also in actions. A ritual action is an action by means of which the divine Mystery is symbolized; the exterior rite reveals and communicates the interior reality. Such is the ritual of the Eucharist. The day before he surrendered his life on the cross Jesus took bread and wine and blessed them and gave them to his disciples in a ritual action which he told them to repeat in memory of him.[8] By this ritual action the mystery of his death and resurrection, of the divine life communicated to men, was symbolized and made present. Here, under the symbols of bread and wine, the divine life is present among men, the eternal Wisdom gives itself to be the food of men, the unutterable mystery of the divine love offering itself in sacrifice to the world is shared in a ritual meal. This in turn is a symbol of the fact that this divine Mystery is present everywhere, present in the earth and its produce, present wherever human beings meet and share together, present in every gesture of unselfish love.

The Church as a visible institution is constituted by the Eucharist. For the Church in this sense is simply the community of those who have recognized the presence of the divine life, of the kingdom of God, in Jesus, and who meet together to share this divine life in the ritual meal which he instituted. But, of course, the divine life is not confined to the Eucharist. It is present everywhere and in everything, in every religion and in every human heart. The Eucharist is the 'sacrament' of the divine life – the outward and visible sign of this divine mystery instituted by Christ – and the Church itself is the 'sacrament' of the kingdom of God, the sign of God's presence on earth. It has the value of a sign, of something which makes known the hidden mystery. The doctrine, the ritual and the organization of the Church all belong to the world of signs, to the sacramental order, which manifests the divine Mystery, the one eternal Truth, by means of human words and actions and a human organization. The danger is that the signs may be taken for the reality, the human may overshadow the

divine, the organization stifle the Spirit which it is intended to serve.

What, then, is the essential Truth which is signified
by the doctrine, the ritual and the organization of the
Church? If we attempt to put it into words we can say
that it is the presence of the divine life among men, of the
infinite, eternal, transcendent mystery of being, which is
the Ground of all religion and of all existence, manifesting itself in the person of Jesus Christ. In this revelation
the mystery of being reveals itself as a mystery of love, of
an eternal love ever rising from the depths of being in the
Godhead and manifesting itself in the total self-giving of
Jesus on the cross and in the communication of that love
to men in the Spirit. The organization of the Church,
with its doctrine of Trinity and Incarnation and its
eucharistic ritual, has no other purpose than to communicate this love, to create a community of love, to
unite all men in the eternal Ground of being, which is
present in the heart of every man. This is the criterion by
which the Church is to be judged, not by the forms of its
doctrine or ritual, but by the reality of the love which it
manifests. Yet though this love must be manifested, it
remains in itself a hidden mystery. It cannot be judged
by any external standards; it can be known only by
those who experience it in themselves. The divine
Mystery will always remain hidden from those who set
up to judge it by rational standards. It always transcends
reason and reveals itself in the depths of the heart.
'Blessed are the pure in heart, for they shall see God.'[9]

The essential nature of the Church, therefore, is to be
this mystery of love, of the divine love revealing itself
and communicating itself to men. All the sign-language
of doctrine and ritual has no purpose but to reveal and
communicate this love. This is the light in which the

doctrine, the ritual and the organization of the Church are to be judged. When the dogmas of the Church, instead of opening the heart and the mind to this mystery of love, become obstacles to the knowledge of the Truth, and people are prepared to imprison and torture and kill one another for the sake of these dogmas, it is obvious that they have ceased to serve their purpose. When the ritual of the Church, instead of being a centre of unity by which people are gathered together in the love of the Spirit, becomes a barrier dividing the different Churches from one another and from the rest of mankind, it has lost its meaning. When the organization of the Church, established in pomp and wealth and power, no longer serves to unite humanity in love, it has ceased to fulfil the purpose for which it was instituted.

What is the answer to this problem? Is it to abolish the Church, to get rid of dogmas, rituals and organization? This is a common temptation, but it never works. It only ends in the substitution of another Church, another dogma, another ritual and another organization. The kingdom of God, the reign of the Spirit, has to take shape in this world. Wherever people share a common ideal, they inevitably form a society, and that society needs some doctrine or ideology to express its purpose, some outward sign to identify it, some organization to hold it together. It is true of the State, of any political party, of a cultural or friendly society, no less than of the Church. No, the organization is necessary, but it has to be continually changed and adapted to changing circumstances in order to serve its original purpose. This is what is required of every religion. It has continually to renew itself. Its dogmas become fixed, its rituals stereotyped, its organization rigid. It has to find new ways of expressing its doctrine to make it meaningful, new forms of ritual which will embody the inner experience of the Spirit, new structures of organization which will respond to the needs of humanity. Every religion today is in the process of renewal. It has to discover again its original message, to define it in the light of the present day, to manifest its power to transform men's lives.

The original message, the essential truth, of every religion is the sacred Mystery, the presence in this world of a hidden Wisdom, which cannot be expressed in words, which cannot be known by sense or reason, but is hidden in the heart – the Ground or Centre or Substance of the soul, of which the mystics speak – and reveals itself to those who seek it in the silence beyond word and thought. All myth and ritual, all doctrine and sacrament, is but a means to awaken the soul to this hidden Mystery, to allow the divine Presence to make itself known. Myth and ritual, word and sacrament, are necessary to make known the Mystery, and therefore every religion has its sacred tradition, its scriptures and its rites, by which the Mystery is revealed. But all these rites and doctrines are liable to become superstitions. The words and the actions remain but the inner meaning is lost or distorted. Every religion has, therefore, to renew itself continually, to rediscover the hidden Mystery to which it is intended to bear witness. The danger in every religion is, on the one hand, a slavish literalism, which clings to the letter or the outward form and loses the inner spirit, and, on the other hand, a crude rationalism, which empties the words and actions of all deeper meaning. The Bible and the Eucharist have both been subjected to this process continually.

SIXTEEN

The Mystery of Nirvana and Brahman

The essential truth of Buddhism is the doctrine of Nirvana. Nirvana is the holy Mystery, the unutterable Truth, the ultimate State. It can only be described by negatives: it is not born, not become, not made, not compounded.[1] It is the cessation of becoming, the cessation of craving, the blowing out of the lamp. It is deathlessness, peace, the unchanging state. All these are but words which point to the inexpressible Truth. But, though it cannot be known, it can be realized. The Buddha is one who has realized this state; he is the enlightened one who has attained the goal, and he teaches the way to the goal. The way is the Dhamma, the noble eightfold path, the way of right view, right thought, right speech, right action, right living, right endeavour, right mindfulness and right contemplation. And the society in which this way is to be found, this goal to be realized, is the Sangha. By having recourse to the Buddha, the Dhamma and the Sangha, one can attain Nirvana, one can realize the ultimate Truth. This is the essential teaching of Buddhism, and though it may appear altogether negative, empty and void, yet because it is essentially a mystical doctrine, it has infinite depth. Because of this the Buddha appears as a being of infinite compassion. Though the story of the Bodhisattva who takes a vow not to enter Nirvana until every soul has been saved comes from a later age, it is a true expression of the original message of the Buddha. Indeed, the whole Mahayana doctrine, with its vast mythology, its com-

plex philosophy and its elaborate techniques of meditation, is an authentic development of the original intuition of the Buddha, just as the elaborate theology and
liturgy and mystical doctrine of the Middle Ages is an
authentic development of the teaching of Christ. The
teaching of the Buddha and the teaching of Christ both
have this infinite depth, because they derive from the
one source, the ultimate Truth, the Ground of being
itself.

The essential truth of Hinduism is the doctrine of the
Brahman. The Brahman is the Mystery of Being, the
ultimate Truth, the one Reality. Yet it also can only be
described by negatives. It is *neti, neti*, not this, not this.[2]
It is unseen, unrelated, inconceivable, uninferable, un-
imaginable, indescribable.[3] Yet though beyond sense
and thought, it is experienced in the depth of the soul as
the very ground of its being. It is the Atman, the Self, the
real being of man as of the universe. 'I am Brahman',[4]
'Thou art that',[5] 'All this [world] is Brahman.'[6] These
are the *mahavakyas*, the 'great sayings', of the Upanishads,
in which the Mystery of Being is revealed. When experienced in this way, it is known as Saccidananda, as
Being, Knowledge, Bliss.[7] It is experienced as absolute
Being (*sat*), the fullness of reality, the one, infinite,
Transcendence. But it is known not by intellect, or by
reason, or by learning; it is known in pure consciousness
(*cit*), a pure intuition in which the knower, the thing
known, and the act of knowing are one. There is here no
duality, all differences have been transcended, there is
only that One 'without a second'. And this is an experience of infinite bliss (*ananda*). All desires are here
fulfilled, the soul has entered into its rest, it attains to
peace – *shanti* – the peace that passes understanding.
This is the supreme goal, the ultimate state, which

the Bhagavad-Gita calls 'the Nirvana of Brahman'.[8]

But one may ask, is this Nirvana of Brahman, like the Nirvana of the Buddha, an impersonal state? It depends what one means by 'person'. If by 'person' one means the self which is shut up in the body, enclosed in this world, occupied with its own thoughts and feelings and appetites and desires, then certainly this self cannot enter Nirvana; it is this self which must die. But if by 'person' one means the Self which is open to the Infinite, to the Eternal, to Truth, to Love, then Nirvana is the realization of this Self, the fulfilment of its being. To enter Nirvana is to become one's self, to become what one really is. It is to behold the Self in all things and all things in the Self.[9] In this sense Nirvana is the most personal of all experiences. That is why at the heart of Buddhism, in spite of its negative doctrine, there is found a person of infinite compassion, the person of the Buddha. That is why Krishna can say, 'He who sees all things in the Self and the Self in all things, sees me in all things and all things in me.'[10] The ultimate Mystery of Being, the Brahman, is revealed not only as the Self of all men, but as the Lord dwelling in the hearts of all men, as an object of worship and of love. The Bhagavad-Gita revealed the Supreme Being as a God of love. 'The Lord dwells in the heart of all beings, O Arjuna . . . In him seek refuge with thy whole soul: by his grace thou shalt win the peace supreme, the everlasting realm.'[11] There is, therefore, no conflict between the personal and the impersonal in the ultimate state. The Brahman, the ultimate Ground of Being, is one with the Atman, the ultimate Ground of the Self, and this in turn is one with the Lord, the personal God. The Person in its ultimate Ground is the eternal Saccidananda, Being in the plenitude of self-knowledge and the perfection of bliss-

ful love – what in Christianity was to be revealed as
Father, Son and Holy Spirit; the Father, the source of
being; the Son, the Word, the wisdom, the manifestation
of the Father; and the Spirit, the blissful love of the
Godhead which is everlasting joy and peace, flowing
from the Father to the Son, and from the Son to the
whole creation.

Of course, all these terms are used in a transcendent
sense. We have to use the method of affirmation, negation
and transcendence. If we say that Brahman is Saccidananda – Being, Knowledge, Bliss – we first of all affirm
that Brahman is Being, absolute Being, Reality itself.
We then go on to deny that Brahman is being in the
same sense as any other being, so that we have to say
that Brahman in a sense is not-being. But finally we say
that Brahman is Being in a transcendent sense, he is
Being in a manner which transcends every mode of
being which we can conceive. It is the same with every
other attribute. Brahman is consciousness – *cit* – but it is
consciousness which transcends any mode of consciousness which we can conceive. Brahman is bliss – *ananda* –
but it is a bliss which transcends any mode of bliss which
we can conceive. In this sense Brahman is called *nirguna*
– 'without attributes'. But this does not mean that
Brahman lacks these attributes of being, consciousness,
bliss, truth, love, but that these attributes exist in him in
a manner that transcends all conceptions. In *saguna*
Brahman – Brahman 'with attributes' – these attributes
are manifested, they become known. In this sense we
can say that *nirguna* Brahman corresponds with the
Father in Christian theology – the ultimate ground of the
Godhead – while *saguna* Brahman corresponds with the
Son, the Word of God, the manifestation of the hidden
Godhead.

Saguna Brahman is manifested in the *trimurti* – the three forms of Brahma, the Creator, Vishnu, the Preserver, and Siva, the Destroyer, but also the Regenerator of the universe. These are the basic forms under which God is worshipped in India, but in practice Brahma is scarcely worshipped at all – he has but one temple in India today – and Vishnu and Siva both alike assume the functions of the Supreme Being. Both alike are worshipped as the one, eternal, infinite transcendent Being manifesting himself to the world. In a sense this is true of all the Hindu gods. Each is a particular manifestation of the one, infinite Transcendence, each is a particular aspect of Brahman. In Hebrew monotheism Yahweh was elevated to the position of the one Supreme God and all other gods were considered first of all as inferior to him, and then as nothing in comparison with him, and finally as demons, that is, powers opposed to him. But Hinduism followed another path. Each of the gods was considered to be a manifestation of the one supreme Reality, the absolute Transcendence, which is 'without a second'. The danger of this is that each particular god may come to be worshipped for himself without reference to the One, and this is properly polytheism. But in Hinduism the tendency has been the opposite. Each god tends to assume all the attributes of the one God, and becomes no more than a name for the one Supreme Being. This is particularly true of Vishnu and Siva, who are simply names of God. It is true also of the Mother-Goddess – the *devi* – who becomes the Sakti of Brahman, the power of the Supreme, and is eventually indistinguishable from the absolute Brahman.

Just as the gods are manifestations of the Brahman, so the whole universe, with everything in it, is a manifestation of Brahman, the one, unutterable Mystery of Being.

The Brahman, as Vishnu, pervades the whole world; every atom, every grain of sand, every blade of grass, is a form of Brahman. As the Upanishad says, 'All this is Brahman.'[12] But is this pantheism? If by pantheism we mean that God is identical with the world and the world with God, then no Hindu system is pantheism. Though Brahman is immanent in all things, it also transcends all things. As the Rig-Veda puts it: 'All creatures are one fourth of him, three fourths are eternal in heaven.'[13] This is putting it crudely, but the meaning is clear. Another way of putting it is to say: 'As the one fire after it has entered the world, though one, becomes different according to whatever it burns, thus the one Self in all things becomes different according to what it enters, and exists also without.'[14] Or again: 'As the one air after it has entered the world, though one, becomes different according to whatever it enters, thus the one Self within all things becomes different according to whatever it enters, and exists also without.'[15] Or again: 'As the sun, the eye of the world, is not contaminated by the external purities seen by the eyes, thus the one Self within all things is not contaminated by the misery of the world, being himself without.'[16] This comes nearer to the truth, but it comes nearest of all when the Brahman, the Self, is compared to a person: There is one ruler, the Self, within all things, who makes the one form manifold. The wise who perceive him within their self, to them belongs happiness, not to others.[17] It is when the Self is recognized intuitively within that the real relation of Brahman to the universe is known, and that cannot properly be expressed in words.

Everything, and every person, exists eternally in Brahman in its uncreated Ground, beyond words and thoughts. This is the ultimate Mystery of Being, which

can only be known when sense and reason are transcended and the Self is known in its eternal ground.
When things and persons come forth into space and
time, then they begin to have a separate existence and
receive name and form. Then they begin to be objects of
sense and thought. But even so, they are wholly per-
vaded by Brahman. They have their being in him and
are only properly known in him. The knowledge of
things and persons in their state of separation apart
from Brahman is *maya*, illusion. This is the ignorance –
avidya – which goes by the name of science today. It is
not altogether false. It is a partial, incomplete knowledge,
a knowledge of appearances which is true as far as it goes.
But when it is mistaken for real knowledge, for the
knowledge of things as they are, it is an illusion. To
know things as they are, one must know one's self; one
must go beyond sense and reason and know the Self in all
things and all things in the Self. This is wisdom, this is
enlightenment, this is to know the Truth.

Every human being is a manifestation of the Brahman,
the one, eternal Self. In so far as he imagines himself to
be a separate being, existing apart from the One, he is a
product of *maya*, a mere illusion. When he comes to
know his true self in the Brahman, then he attains enlightenment. As the Upanishad says: Two birds, in-
separable friends, cling to the same tree. One of these
eats the fruit, the other looks on without eating.[18] The
two birds are the individual soul – the *jivatman* – and the
supreme Self – the *Paramatman*. The individual soul
eats the fruit of this world and gets entangled in *maya*,
thinking itself a separate being. But when it recognizes
the other, the true Self, who is also the Lord, then it is set
free. This beautiful parable shows the true nature of
the soul. It is a temporal manifestation of the one, eternal

Self. When it forgets its true nature and gets immersed in this world, it is full of misery, but when it recognizes its true Self, in the Lord, dwelling in the heart, then it attains to peace. In Christian terms we can say that when the soul turns to God and is united with him, it finds its true self, its real being, and is freed from the illusion of sin. Or going deeper, we can say that the Spirit of God dwells in the heart of every man. When we recognize this Spirit as our true Self, the life of our soul, the breath of our being, then we are united with the Lord, with Christ the Saviour, and through him attain to the peace of the Father.

The Father is *nirguna* Brahman, the naked Godhead, the abyss of Being, the divine darkness, without form and void, the silence where no word is spoken, where no thought comes, the absolute nothingness from which everything comes, the not-being from which all being comes, the One without a second, which is utterly empty yet immeasurably full, wayless and fathomless,[19] beyond the reach of thought. He cannot be named, cannot be expressed, cannot be conceived. The Son is *saguna* Brahman, the Word, through whom the Father receives a name, by which he is expressed, by which he is conceived. The Son is the manifestation of the Father, his Image and Likeness, making known the hidden depths of the Godhead. In the Son the whole creation comes forth eternally from the Father. Everything that is hidden in the abyss of the Godhead comes to light in him. He is the light in which everything is known and receives name and form. He is God 'with attributes', revealing the power, the wisdom, the glory, the life, the light, the truth, the love, which is hidden in the Father. He is the consciousness (*cit*) of the Father, expressing his being, the Self in which he eternally reflects himself and makes himself known. Each of us comes forth eternally from the hidden depths of the Father into being in the Word. There we receive name and form. There we are known from all eternity. In the Father we exist from all eternity in an unfathomable unity of being without distinction. In the Son we exist eternally in distinction of being, and yet without distinction, because in God all creatures are God.[20] This is our eternal uncreated being in the Word. But when we come into being in time, then we become distinct and separate. Then we come to exist not simply in God but in ourselves. Yet even so, the grace of God is always drawing us back to himself. We come forth from God in order that we may exist in ourselves and know ourselves as distinct and separate, each a distinct and unique reflection of God, with a capacity of freedom, a power to choose and to will our own being. It is then that we can choose to separate ourselves from God, to refuse to recognize our dependence on God, to create an illusory independence and become subject to *maya*. Or we can choose to return to God, to find our real being in him, to know ourselves as expressions of his being, as manifestations of his Word. This is the drama of sin and redemption.

Each of us has in the ultimate ground of his being an eternal being in the Father, beyond word and thought, hidden in the darkness, in the uncreated Source of being, where no creature appears, no distinction is known. And each of us has an eternal being in the Son, where we come into being from the Father, each a unique manifestation of the one Word of God, each a unique image and reflection of his being, distinct from all others as a living idea in the mind of God, yet inseparably one with God, sharing the divine nature. Again, each of us has a separate, finite existence, in which we are separated from God, fallen from the divine life, shut up in this world of matter, divided by space and time and imprisoned in ourselves. But finally, each of us has an existence in which we are being called to return to God, to awaken to the divine life within us, to respond to the movement of the Spirit, to listen to the voice of the Word, to recover our divine nature and finally to return to the Father, to lose ourselves in that abyss of Being from which we came. For in that abyss of Being, in that Nirvana of Brahman, everything that has come forth not only in time but in eternity, the divine Saccidananda, Father, Son and Holy Spirit, is found in the absolute plenitude of Being, which is yet so far beyond thought that it appears to us as a darkness, a void, an abyss of nothingness.

SEVENTEEN

The Mystery of the Spirit

We come forth from the Father in the Son and we return to the Father in the Spirit. The Spirit is the Sakti – the power – of the Godhead, the breath by which the Word is uttered, the energy which flows from the Father into the Word and overflows in the creation. It is by the Spirit that the 'ideas' in the Word are given form and substance and the creation comes into being. 'The Spirit of God was moving over the face of the waters.'[1] The Spirit is the feminine principle in the Godhead, the Mother of all creation. It is in her that the seeds of the Word are planted and she nurtures them and brings them forth in creation. The Spirit is the source of energy in the stars and atoms, of life in plants and animals. It is the source of evolution in the universe. It is the Spirit in man which first gives us life – the Lord God 'breathed into his nostrils the breath of life; and man became a living being'[2] and then awakens consciousness in us. It is the Spirit which is continually drawing us into the divine life. For the Spirit is that divine life latent in the universe from the beginning, latent in nature and becoming concious in us. By the Spirit we know that we are not merely flesh and blood, formed from the matter of the universe, not merely the subject of sensations, feelings, imaginations and thoughts, but an energy of love which seeks always to transcend the barriers of space and time and to discover the divine life. The Spirit is this energy of love in us, this power of the divine. It is the Source of our real being, by which we become conscious of the divine life in us and know ourselves as sons of God.

The Spirit is the Atman, the Self, which dwells in the heart of every creature. It is this Spirit of which it is said: 'It is not born, it does not die; it sprang from nothing, nothing sprang from it. It is the ancient, unborn, eternal, everlasting. It is not killed though the body is killed. It is smaller than the small, greater than the great. Though sitting still, he walks far; though lying down, he goes everywhere. He is bodiless within bodies, unchanging among things that change.'[3] 'It is inside all this and it is outside all this.'[4] The Spirit is one in everyone and in everything. It is ever the same, yet it appears different, just as the light of the sun is ever the same but appears in different colours according to the nature of the thing in which it shines. So the Spirit manifests in each thing according to its capacity to receive it. It is energy, light and heat in the sun and the stars, life in plants and animals, consciousness in man. It adapts itself to the capacity of every man. It is the speed of the athlete, the skill of the artist, the imagination of the poet, the intelligence of the philosopher, the wisdom of the seer. Or rather it is the Source of all these things, containing all power in itself and remaining for ever unchanged. The life of the body, the thoughts and feelings of the soul, are alike the effects of the Spirit in man. It is the source of our very individuality, what makes us capable of judgement and choice and decision, the principle of freedom and responsibility. In every man the same Spirit is present, adapting itself to his capacities. Of this Spirit it is said: '[She] is more mobile than any motion; because of her pureness she pervades and penetrates all things.'[5]

We must be careful to distinguish between the soul

and the Spirit. The soul is the *jivatman*, the source of our separate existence, of our individual being. It is what Aristotle calls the 'form' of the body, that which gives life to the body and determines us to a bodily existence. But the soul is also the source of reason and free will, by which it is open to the Spirit, the *Paramatman*. The Spirit is the source of unity and universality, the soul of diversity and individuality. If the soul identifies itself with the body, it becomes enclosed in its separate existence, but if it opens itself to the Spirit, it can transcend its separate individuality and realize its identity with the Spirit. When the soul identifies itself with the body, man becomes the natural or 'psychic' man of St Paul,[6] who lives 'according to the flesh';[7] when the soul identifies itself with the Spirit, it becomes the spiritual man, who lives 'according to the Spirit'.[8] This identification takes place through the activity of the mind and the will, either accepting the 'law of the flesh' and submitting to the appetites and desires, or accepting the 'law of the Spirit' and allowing itself to be transformed. When the soul submits to the law of the flesh, though it appears to be acting freely, it is really subjecting itself to the law of nature – to *prakriti*, to the law of *karma* – so that it becomes bound by its actions. When it submits to the law of the Spirit, it becomes passive to the action of the Spirit. The mind and the will become instruments of the Spirit. But it is not a forced submission imposed from without; it is a free and loving submission, the Spirit working from within, confirming the judgement of the mind and establishing the freedom of the will. In fact, the Spirit is the source of all the action, both of the body and of the soul, but when the soul refuses to acknowledge this and asserts its own independence, it blocks the free movement of the Spirit and blinds its own judgement.

When the veil of egoism is taken away, it opens itself to the light of the Spirit and allows it to act freely.

But what is the exact relation of the soul to the Spirit? The Upanishads speak of two birds on one tree, of which one eats the fruit, while the other looks on without eating.[9] The first is the *jivatman*, the individual soul, which eats the fruit of this world and becomes subject to the law of nature, of birth and death. The second is the *Paramatman*, the supreme Spirit, which is ever one and the same, the silent witness of the activity of the soul. When the soul looks up and beholds the Spirit, the eternal Ground of its being, who is also the Lord, the Creator, it is released from the bondage to nature and becomes one with the Spirit. As St Paul says: 'He who is united to the Lord becomes one spirit with him.'[10] But does the soul then become God? It depends what one means by 'becoming God'. Obviously, the relation between God and the soul, or between *jivatman* and *Paramatman*, cannot properly be expressed, because one of the terms is the absolute Transcendence which is beyond our comprehension. Sankara[11] evades the difficulty by saying that the *jivatman* has no real existence. It is a mere appearance of the one, eternal Spirit, with no more reality than the form of a snake which is mistakenly imposed on a piece of rope. The rope – the *Paramatman* – is the one reality; the snake – the appearance of the *jivatman* – is the product of *maya*. The soul in reality is the Spirit and there is no essential difference between them. Ramanuja says that the soul in *moksha*, that is, in its final state of liberation, is joined to the Lord without ceasing to be different from him, and enjoys an intuitive vision of the supreme Spirit.[12] Madhva will only say that the soul, which is eternally different from God, comes to dwell with him and has continual sight of him.[13] Saiva

Siddhanta comes, perhaps, nearest to a Christian view when it says that the soul by grace shares in the very nature of Siva, the supreme God, and becomes one with him in love without losing its individuality.[14]

What, then, is the Christian view of this relationship? We have to say that originally the soul exists in God in an absolute identity of being beyond all distinctions.[15] When the soul comes into being in the Word, as an eternal idea in the mind of God, it still has no separate being. As Aquinas says, the 'ideas' in God by which he knows all possible and existent beings are identical with the divine being.[16] They are distinct not in reality (*in re*) but only in conception (*ratione*). It is only when the Spirit of God, his eternal will and energy, gives existence to the soul, that it begins to have a separate being. Even so, all that the soul has of being comes wholly from the Spirit, it has nothing of itself at all. All that the soul has of itself is its limitation of being, which is determined by the body which it informs. The one Spirit, therefore, which is ever one and the same – the *Paramatman* – is present to every soul, giving it existence, sustaining it in existence and drawing it into union with itself. In other words, in each one of us there is a soul which gives 'form' to the matter of the body, which determines us to a bodily existence and which is subject to all the passions of the body. But in each of us there is also a presence of the Spirit, which gives existence to the soul as well as to the body – for the Spirit is present in every particle of matter, giving it existence and form and substance – which watches over the soul, inspires and directs its mind and will, and enables it to awaken to its source of being in the Spirit and to be transformed by its power. But what is this transformation? The soul discovers its source of being in the Spirit, the mind is opened to this inner light, the will is energized by this inner power. The very substance of the soul is changed; it is made a 'partaker of the divine nature'.[17] And this transformation affects not only the soul but also the body. The matter of the body – its actual particles – is transformed by the divine power and transfigured by the divine light – like the body of Christ at the resurrection. This is the 'divinization' of man, which will be manifested in the resurrection of all men. 'We shall all be changed, in a moment, in the twinkling of an eye, at the last trumpet. For the trumpet will sound, and the dead will be raised imperishable, and we shall be changed. For this perishable nature must put on the imperishable, and this mortal nature must put on immortality.'[18]

This is *moksha*, this is final release, but it is not a release from the body or the soul, but the taking up of body and soul into the life of the Spirit. Both body and soul here realize all their potentialities. Matter, according to Aristotle, is potentiality. It has no being in itself, only an infinite capacity for being. It is Spirit which gives being and actuality to matter, building up the stellar universe and the innumerable forms of life, drawing out the infinite potentiality of matter into ever new forms of being. In the human being matter transcends itself, it emerges into consciousness. The Spirit working within matter draws this new mode of being from the potentiality of matter. But our present mode of consciousness determined by the present state of our bodily existence is only a transitional phase in the evolution of matter. The presence of psychic powers in human nature which transcend our normal consciousness is already evidence of this. Extra-sensory perception, telepathy, thought-reading, foreseeing the future, appearing at a distance, spiritual healing in various ways, are all now well attested. In the science of Yoga there are various powers, or *siddhis*, by which the control of the mind over the body and the expansion of the powers of the mind can be developed.[19] But all this is only a foretaste of that radical transformation of the matter of the body which will take place in the resurrection.

EIGHTEEN

Yoga, the Way of Union

The transformation of body and soul by the Spirit is the work of Yoga. In the classical system of Patanjali there are two principles which govern not only human life but the whole creation. One is the masculine principle, Purusha, who is pure consciousness, the other is the feminine principle, Prakriti, who is the source of all the activity of nature. The cause of all suffering in this world is that *purusha*, consciousness, has become entangled with *prakriti* and become subject to the passions of nature. The art of Yoga is to separate *purusha* from *prakriti*, consciousness from the actions and passions of nature, so that the consciousness becomes free from every movement of nature and enjoys the bliss of pure contemplation, untouched by any taint of mortality. This ideal of *kaivalya*, of total separation from the world, has been present in Hinduism from early times, and for Sankara this remains the goal of life. All the activity of nature is *maya*; it is an illusion due to ignorance. Wisdom consists of the knowledge of being in pure consciousness without any modification, and this brings lasting bliss – *saccidananda* — the bliss of the pure consciousness of being. There is certainly profound truth in this doctrine. There is an experience of being in pure consciousness which gives lasting peace to the soul. It is an experience of the Ground or Depth of being in the Centre of the soul, an awareness of the mystery of being beyond sense and thought, which gives a sense of fulfilment, of finality, of absolute truth. And indeed there is a sense in which this experience is ultimate. It is an experience of the undifferentiated Ground of being, the Abyss of being beyond thought, the One without a second. But does this mean that all other modes of consciousness are illusory, that nature has no reality, that the experience of God is also an illusion?

Though Sankara has many followers among Hindus today, his doctrine has never gained universal acceptance. It has been opposed from the beginning by the Vaishnava philosophers, who were devoted to a personal God, Ramanuja, Madhva, Nimbarka, Vallabha and Caitanya, who have constructed rival systems of Vedanta in opposition to Sankara, and it is rejected by Saiva Siddhanta. Moreover, in modern times it has met with opposition from those philosophers who under the influence of the West have recognized the values of matter and life, of history and personality, of whom Sri Aurobindo is the greatest. In his philosophy[1] there is a wonderful synthesis, based on the Vedanta, of ancient and modern thought. In him the values of being and becoming, of spirit and matter, of the One and the many, of the eternal and the temporal, of the universal and the individual, of the personal God and the absolute Godhead, are integrated in a vision of the whole, which has never been surpassed in depth and comprehensiveness. In the integral yoga of Sri Aurobindo the values of matter and life and human consciousness and the experience of a personal God are not lost in the ultimate Reality, the divine Saccidananda. Matter and life and consciousness in man are seen to be evolving towards the divine life and the divine consciousness, in which they are not annihilated but fulfilled.

This is the goal of a Christian yoga. Body and soul are

to be transfigured by the divine life and to participate in the divine consciousness. There is a descent of the Spirit into matter and a corresponding ascent, by which matter is transformed by the indwelling power of the Spirit and the body is transfigured. In Kundalini Yoga this is represented as the union of Siva and Sakti in the human body. The divine power is represented as coiled up like a serpent at the base of the spine. This divine energy has to be led through the seven *chakras*, or centres of psychic energy, until it reaches the thousand-petalled lotus at the crown of the head. Then Siva, who is pure consciousness, unites with Sakti, the divine energy in nature, and body and soul are transformed. This is very different from the Yoga of Patanjali, where consciousness (*purusha*) is separated from nature (*prakriti*) and enjoys the bliss of isolation (*kaivalya*). Yet both these yogas have their place. There must be a movement of ascent to pure consciousness, a detachment from all the moods of nature, a realization of the Self in its eternal Ground beyond space and time. But then there must also be a movement of descent, by which the Spirit enters into the depths of matter and raises it to a new mode of existence, in which it becomes the medium of a spiritual consciousness.

For a Christian this has already taken place in the resurrection of Christ. In his body matter has already been transformed, so as to become a spiritual body, which is the medium of the divine life. The human body by contact with this body of Christ, which is no longer limited by space and time, has within it the seed of the divine life. As St Paul says: 'We ourselves, who have the first fruits of the Spirit, groan inwardly as we wait for . . . the redemption of our bodies.'[2] And this 'groaning' is part of the travail of all nature, which waits to be delivered 'from its bondage to decay and obtain the glorious liberty of the children of God'.[3] This is the cosmic drama, this transformation of nature, of matter and the body, so as to become the outward form of the divine Spirit, the body of the Lord. And this transformation is taking place in our own bodies. In every human being matter is being transformed daily into Spirit. We take in matter through our bodies as food, and that matter goes to feed the brain, and the brain produces thought. Thought itself is matter become Spirit. But for most of us this process remains incomplete. Matter is never fully assimilated by Spirit, and at death the matter unassimilated by the Spirit returns to the earth. But in the body of Christ we can see that transformation of matter by Spirit taking place, which is the destiny of us all at the end of time. The body of the Virgin Mary is said to have been transformed in the same way, and doubtless there are other saints and yogis of whom this is true.

The real end of Yoga, then, is the transformation of body and soul by the power of the indwelling Spirit, the Atman. In the classical system of Patanjali there are eight stages in this process of transformation. The first two stages – *yama* and *niyama* – give the moral basis without which any yoga is useless. They consist of obedience to the commandments – not to kill, not to steal, to adhere to the truth, to preserve chastity, not to covet. After these come the counsels – cleanliness or purity of mind and body, contentment, in the sense of equanimity in the face of the opposites, good and evil, pleasure and pain, joy and sorrow. Then asceticism or self-control, meditation on the scriptures and devotion to God. This is the basic pattern of moral and spiritual life, which is common to all religions. The next two stages –

asana and *pranayama* – are the practice of bodily posture and control of the breath, which are particularly associated with Yoga. These are, in fact, the methods of Hatha Yoga, which aims at the transformation of body and soul by bodily exercise, and the acquisition of *siddhis* – that is, the yogic powers which result from complete control over the body. The next four stages are the stages of meditation, first recollection (*pratyahara*), then concentration (*dharana*), then meditation itself or 'the unbroken flow of thought towards the object of concentration', and finally *samadhi* – the absorption of the mind in the object of its contemplation, when all sense of the distinction of subject and object disappears. But all these are only techniques by which soul and body are brought into subjection to the Spirit and the soul awakens to the divine life within.

Apart from the classical system of Yoga, or Raja Yoga, there are three ways of Yoga, the way of action (*karma*), the way of devotion (*bhakti*) and the way of knowledge (*jnana*). There are not many who can follow the way of body-control and mind-control of the classical system. For most people the way to self-discovery, to union with God, is by action. This was the great discovery of the Bhagavad-Gita. At first it was thought that the way to union with God, the path of salvation, was to be found in the practice of asceticism, in silence and solitude, in prolonged meditation. But the Bhagavad-Gita declared that the householder doing the ordinary duties of his life could attain salvation no less than the ascetic in the forest. Man could be saved by work: all that was required was that the work should be done with detachment.[4] It is work which is done with attachment, that is, with selfish motives, that binds the soul. We must not seek the 'fruit' of work. We have to make the offering of the work to God, then it is no longer we who act but God who acts in us. The lower self, the ego, must be sacrificed; the action must come from the higher Self, the Spirit in us, then it becomes a holy action. This is the way in which we awake to the presence of the Spirit in us. It does not matter what the work may be, whether it is manual or intellectual, work of organization, of management, of service or of prayer. It has to be done with detachment, it has to be offered to God. Every poet knows this. The poem cannot be manufactured, it has to come from the Self within. In this sense all work is poetry, and should have the seal of beauty, which is the seal of the Spirit, on it.

The second way is the way of devotion, of love for a personal God. This is the second great principle of the Bhagavad-Gita. In the Upanishads the Godhead was conceived as the Brahman, the one, absolute, transcendent Being, beyond word and thought. But this Brahman was also the Atman, the Self, the Ground of human consciousness. It was not only Being but Knowledge and Bliss. But to speak of a being who is knowledge and bliss is to imply a personal being, for a person is simply a conscious being, a being possessed of intelligence and will. Very soon this becomes explicit and the Self was described as God, the Lord, in directly personal terms.[5] Of course, the word 'person' is used by analogy, like all terms which are applied to the Godhead. A human person is a finite being possessing a finite intellect and a finite will. When applied to the infinite being of the Godhead, it can only mean that in the Godhead there is an infinite capacity for knowledge and love, analogous to our human capacity but infinitely transcending it. And this is not only speculation. In the experience of *bhakti*, in the total surrender of the intellect and the will to the infinite Transcendence, there is an experience of personal relationship; the intellect is illuminated by the eternal light and the will transfigured by the infinite love. This is the experience of the mystics of all religions. Of course, human language fails here, because we are passing beyond the barriers of human nature. The God who is experienced in mystical ecstasy is more than personal and can be described in impersonal terms, as Light, Life, Truth, Beauty, Being itself. But this transcendent Being is more, not less, than personal, and therefore it is misleading to describe it as impersonal. In the Christian doctrine of the Trinity, the Godhead is the one, absolute, infinite, transcendent Mystery of Being beyond word and thought, but within this being there is revealed the plenitude of personal being, of wisdom and love, transcending all human conception, but realized in the fullness of personal relationship, more meaningful than any human knowledge and more real than any human love. To realize this relationship of knowledge and love in one's self by total surrender to the divine love is the way of *bhakti*. 'If a man loves me, he will keep my word, and my Father will love him, and we will come to him and make our home with him.'[6]

Finally, there is the way of knowledge (*jnana*), of wisdom. This is the knowledge of the Self, the Atman, the true Being. It is not a knowledge which can be acquired by reason, or by learning, or even through the scriptures.[7] It is a knowledge which comes from above. The path to it is by *metanoia*, by repentance, by turning back, by a return to the source. There must be a radical detachment from the self, that is, from all selfish attachment to the world, the flesh and the ego. The self, the *jivatman*, must be surrendered. It must become completely empty, void, dead to itself. This is the difficult crossing, the passage to the other shore, the passing away. Unless the grain of wheat die, it cannot bear fruit.[8] He who will lose his life shall save it.[9] This is the great paradox behind all life. All methods of meditation are intended to lead to this point. The mind must die to itself, to its concepts, its reason. The surface mind must cease its activity, all thought must cease. Then in the silence, in the stillness, beyond thought, a deeper mind becomes known, the true Self begins to emerge. This is the *Paramatman*, the supreme Self, the light of the Word, shining in the heart. By this light all is enlightened,[10] by this everything is known.[11] This is the end of the journey; beyond this it is impossible to go. For here the human passes into the divine, the temporal into the eternal, the finite into the infinite. What words can describe this state, what thought penetrate it? It is the ultimate mystery.

Yet something can be said about it, if only to say what it is not. Does it mean that man becomes God, or that God disappears together with man, and the One alone remains? There is a sense in which both these statements are true. Surely, in a sense, that man should become God is the end alike of creation and redemption. Did not the great Athanasius say: God became man that man might become God? Did not Jesus pray that 'they may all be one; even as thou, Father, art in me, and I in thee, that they also may be in us'?[12] Are we not made 'partakers of the divine nature'?[13] But how are we to understand this? Man is not divine by nature: by nature he is poor and weak and sinful, thrown upon this world and struggling for existence. His 'divinization' is the work of grace. The Spirit descends and 'informs' the matter of the body, transforms him from within. He has to free himself from his attachment to matter, to the body, and surrender himself to the action of the Spirit. Then the Spirit transforms both body and soul, re-creates them in the image of God.[14] Then, when this image has been restored to the divine likeness, the light of the Word shines in it.[15] It is now like a mirror from which every speck of dust has been removed, so that the Word reflects itself in it. This Word is the express image of God, in which the plenitude of the Godhead is reflected,[16] and each human being, each particular image, reflects this divine light according to its capacity. To know the Self, to become Brahman, is to know the supreme Self reflected in the individual self. It is to know this Self, to become this Self, to be transformed into this Self, but it is not to comprehend the Self. No man can ever comprehend God: even Jesus in his human nature could not comprehend God. Even in the beatific vision the infinity of the Godhead remains beyond our reach. It is like measuring the ocean. We are plunged in the ocean, we are immersed in it, the drop of water is dissolved in it, but still we cannot comprehend it. The Word alone comprehends the Father.

But in what sense can we say that God and the world 'disappear' in this ultimate state? The soul has to die to this world, to the body, to itself, when it passes over into the divine life. It has to die to its created nature, but it lives in God and through God and for God. It has become part of the ocean, but it does not therefore cease to exist. As St Francis of Sales said: 'Suppose a drop of water, thrown into an ocean of orange water, were alive and could speak, would it not cry out in great joy: "True, I am living, yet it is not myself who lives, but this ocean lives in me, and my soul is hidden away in its depths"? The soul that flows into God does not die, for how could she die through being drowned in life? Rather, she lives by not living in herself.' This is the death of the soul, which is its eternal life. But what of God, does he survive this death, this passing away? If we mean by God a being who stands over against man, the Lord, the Creator, the Other, then it is hard to see how this God can survive. The soul has passed beyond this present mode of consciousness, beyond its created being. The distinction, as we now understand it, between God and the soul has been transcended. It is not God who remains but the Godhead, not 'saguna Brahman', God with attributes, related to man, but 'nirguna Brahman', God without attributes, the absolute Transcendence, the Abyss of the Godhead. We have returned to the Source, to the Ground of being, to the One 'without a second'. Yet in this Ground, in this Source, everything is contained, everything is there, God and the soul, and the body and the universe, but in a manner beyond our conception, where all differences and distinctions, as we understand them, are transcended. This is the peace that passes understanding, the Nirvana of Brahman, the Emptiness, the Nothingness, where thought ceases and all is still. But in that stillness, in that silence, the Word is hidden, the Word in which everything exists eternally in the plenitude of being. And in that Word the Spirit is present, the Spirit which is in all creation and in the heart of every man, and in our own inmost being. And that Spirit is Love, a love which penetrates every atom in the universe, which fills every living thing, which moves the heart of every man, which gathers all into unity. In that Spirit we are all one in the Word, each one unique in himself, reflecting the light of the Word, and in that Word we are one with the Father, the Source of all. 'That they may all be one; even as thou, Father, art in me, and I in thee, that they also may be in us.'[17] This is our destiny, to be one with God in a unity which transcends all distinctions, and yet in which each individual being is found in his integral wholeness.

NOTES

1. A 'SANNYASI' IN INDIA

1. Matthew 10:9–10; 8:20.
2. *Rule of St Benedict*, ch. 33.
3. Romans 12:1.
4. 1 Corinthians 6:13.
5. cf. Bhagavad-Gita, 11.72.

2. THE SACRED MYSTERY

1. cf. *Katha* Upanishad, 4.1.
2. John 8:32.
3. cf. Mircea Eliade, *Patterns in Comparative Religion* (Sheed & Ward, London, 1971), ch. 10.
4. *Brhadaranyaka* Upanishad, III.8.11.
5. J. R. Swanton, quoted in Christopher Dawson's *Progress and Religion* (Sheed & Ward, London, 1929, and Greenwood Press, Westport, Conn., 1970), ch. 4.
6. Riggs, quoted ibid.
7. *Dhammapada*, xx.5–7, literally, 'all things are impermanent (*anicca*), all are sorrowful (*dukkha*), all are without a self (*anatta*).'
8. Ecclesiastes 1:2.
9. *Udana*, 80–1. From the Pali canon of Hinayana Buddhism.
10. ibid.
11. Luke 23:43.
12. Sankara (8th century AD) taught the doctrine of 'non-dualism': the ultimate Reality is *advaita* – without duality.
13. cf. Aquinas, *Summa Theologica*, I.xv.1. ad 3.
14. *Tao Te Ching*, 1.
15. cf. Dionysius the Areopagite, *Mystical Theology*.

16. cf. *Brhadaranyaka* Upanishad, 11.4.13.
17. From the *Prajnaparamitahrdaya* Sutra, the 'perfect wisdom' of Mahayana Buddhism. '*Gate, gate, paragate, parasamgate, bodhi, svaha.*'

3. THE REVELATION OF THE MYSTERY

1. cf. Ignatius of Antioch, *Letter to the Magnesians*, VIII.2.
2. *Tao Te Ching*, XXV.
3. Bhagavad-Gita, XIV.4.
4. ibid, 11.22.
5. *Summa Theologica*, 1a.11ae.81.1.
6. Ephesians 1:9–10.
7. Ramanuja, Commentary on *Vedanta* Sutras.
8. Colossians 2:9.
9. Genesis 1:2.
10. 1 Corinthians 15:45.

4. WHO AM I?

1. Sakti is the divine power represented in Hinduism as the feminine aspect of the deity.
2. cf. Psalm 104:30.
3. Psalm 33:9.
4. Commentary on *Chandogya* Upanishad.
5. John 17:23.

5. THE ONE AND THE MANY

1. From the *Duino Elegies* (Hogarth Press, London, 1939), Appendix IV.
2. 1 Corinthians 15:52–3.
3. The definition of Boethius, quoted by Aquinas, *Summa Theologica*, 1.X.1.
4. Sankara, Commentary on *Brahma* Sutra.
5. The invocation to the *Isa* Upanishad.

6. SIN AND REDEMPTION

1. 1 Corinthians 15:22.
2. 2 Corinthians 5:19.
3. 1 Corinthians 15:24, 28.

7. THE COSMIC POWERS

1. Matthew 16:18, 23.

8. THE MYSTERY OF LOVE

1. From the *Lankavatara* Sutra of Mahayana Buddhism.
2. *Svetasvatara* Upanishad, III.20.
3. The male and female organs.
4. Purusha is the Male, who is pure consciousness. Prakriti is Nature, the feminine aspect of being.
5. John 1:13.
6. *Brhadaranyaka* Upanishad, II.4.5.
7. Hebrews 11:10.

9. THE ULTIMATE TRUTH

1. Matthew 18:3.
2. *Katha* Upanishad, 2.5–6.

10. THE ONE SPIRIT IN ALL RELIGION

1. Ephesians 3:9; cf. Romans 16:25.

11. MYTH AND REALITY

1. Matthew 12:40.
2. *Katha* Upanishad, 3.10–11.

12. THE BUDDHA, KRISHNA AND CHRIST

1. Bhagavad-Gita, xviii.65.
2. Matthew 20:28.
3. Bhagavad-Gita, x.12.
4. Ephesians 1:10.

13. DEATH AND RESURRECTION

1. cf. *Katha* Upanishad, 6.2.
2. Bhagavad-Gita, xi.32.
3. Hebrews 12:29.
4. cf. Psalm 66:3.
5. Exodus 34:6.
6. Matthew 11:28-9.
7. Matthew 25:41.
8. Matthew 5:28.
9. Galatians 6:14.
10. Galatians 2:20.
11. cf. *Isa* Upanishad, 1.
12. Quoted in Erich Heller's *The Disinherited Mind* (3rd ed., Bowes & Bowes, London, and Barnes & Noble, New York, 1971).

14. THE ETERNAL RELIGION

1. Romans 2:15.
2. William Law, *The Spirit of Prayer*, ch. 11.
3. Matthew 13:44-6.
4. Luke 10:42.
5. cf. J. Daniélou, *Holy Pagans of the Old Testament* (Longmans, Green, London, 1957).
6. cf. Mircea Eliade, *Patterns in Comparative Religion*, ch. 2.
7. cf. *Chandogya* Upanishad, viii.1.3.
8. John 1:4, according to one reading.
9. *Katha* Upanishad, 4.1.
10. ibid., 2.23; cf. *Mundaka* Upanishad, iii.2.3.

11. *Katha* Upanishad, 3.13. The 'knowing Self' is the intellect, the *buddhi*, the Nous of Aristotle. The 'great Self' is the *mahat*, the cosmic consciousness, the 'divine soul' of Plotinus. The 'Self of peace' is the supreme Self, the *Paramatman*, the Word of God.

12. Al-Ghazali (d. AD 1111): cf. A. J. Arberry's *Sufism* (Allen & Unwin, London, 1950, and Harper & Row, New York, 1970).

13. Nagarjuna (*c.* AD 150), founder of the Madhyamika school of Mahayana Buddhism, with its doctrine of the Void (*sunyata*).

14. Vasubandhu (*c.* AD 400), founder of the Yogacara school of Mahayana Buddhism, with its doctrine of 'mind only': cf. E. Conze's *Buddhism* (Cassirer, Oxford 1951).

15. Mark 1:15.

16. *Svetasvatara* Upanishad, III.20.

17. From the *Lankavatara* Sutra.

18. Leviticus 26:12.

19. Koran, L.16.

20. John 2:19, 21.

21. cf. Ephesians 1:22; 2:20; 4:15–16.

22. Ephesians 3:19.

15. THE CHRISTIAN MYSTERY

1. cf. Matthew 11:27; Luke 10:22.

2. John 17:5, 24.

3. John 14:10.

4. cf. John 15:26.

5. cf. John 17:11.

6. cf. Hebrews 4:15.

7. cf. John 14:9.

8. cf. 1 Corinthians 11:23–6.

9. Matthew 5:8.

16. THE MYSTERY OF NIRVANA AND BRAHMAN

1. *Udana*, 80–1; cf. chapter 2, note 9.
2. *Brhadaranyaka* Upanishad, 11.3.6.
3. *Mandukya* Upanishad, 7.
4. cf. *Brhadaranyaka* Upanishad, 1.4.10.
5. cf. *Chandogya* Upanishad, v1.8.7.
6. cf. ibid., 111.14.1.
7. cf. *Brhadaranyaka* Upanishad, 111.9.28.
8. Bhagavad-Gita, v.24.
9. cf. ibid., v1.29.
10. ibid., v1.30.
11. ibid., xv111.61–2.
12. *Chandogya* Upanishad, 111.14.1.
13. Rig-Veda, x.90.
14. *Katha* Upanishad, 5.9.
15. ibid., 5.10.
16. ibid., 5.11.
17. ibid., 5.12.
18. *Svetasvatara* Upanishad, iv.6.
19. cf. Ruysbroeck, *The Adornment of the Spiritual Marriage*, bk. 11, ch. LXIV.
20. cf. Eckhart: 'If we say that all things are in God, we understand by this that, just as he is without distinction in his nature yet absolutely distinct from all things, so all things are in him in the greatest distinction and yet not distinct, and first of all because man is God in God . . .' (Latin Sermon iv.1.). cf. also Ruysbroeck, *The Adornment of the Spiritual Marriage*, bk. 111 ch. 111: 'In eternity all creatures are God in God.'

17. THE MYSTERY OF THE SPIRIT

1. Genesis 1:2.
2. Genesis 2:7.
3. *Katha* Upanishad, 2.18.22.
4. *Isa* Upanishad, 5.
5. Wisdom of Solomon 7:24.
6. cf. 1 Corinthians 2:14.
7. Romans 8:4.

8. ibid.
9. *Svetasvatara* Upanishad, IV.6.
10. 1 Corinthians 6:17.
11. Sankara (8th century AD), author of the doctrine of *advaita*, or non-duality, taught that reality is one, absolute, undifferentiated being 'without duality' (*a-dvaita*), and that all differences are an appearance – *maya* – superimposed on this one being.
12. Ramanuja (11th century AD) was the author of the doctrine of *visishtadvaita*, 'qualified non-duality', which maintains that God stands to the world in the relation of soul to body.
13. Madhva (13th century AD), author of the doctrine of *dvaita*, or 'duality', taught that God, the soul and the world are all really different from one another.
14. Saiva Siddhanta is the doctrine of the Southern school of Saivism (13th century AD), which claims to be the perfection of all the schools of Vedanta.
15. cf. chapter 17, note 20.
16. *Summa Theologica*, XV.1. ad 3.
17. 2 Peter 1:4.
18. 1 Corinthians 15:51–3.
19. cf. Patanjali, *Yoga-sutras*, bk. III.

18. YOGA, THE WAY OF UNION

1. cf. esp. *The Life Divine* (2nd ed., Arya Publishing House, Calcutta, 1944, and Sri Aurobindo Library, New York, 1951) and *The Synthesis of Yoga* (Sri Aurobindo Library, Madras, 1948).
2. Romans 8:23.
3. Romans 8:21.
4. cf. Bhagavad-Gita, esp. bks. 11–VI.
5. cf. *Brhadaranyaka* Upanishad, IV.4.15.
6. John 14:23.
7. cf. *Katha* Upanishad, 2.23; and *Mundaka* Upanishad, III.2.3.
8. John 12:24.
9. Matthew 16:25.
10. *Svetasvatara* Upanishad, VI.14.

11. cf. *Mundaka* Upanishad, 1.1.3.
12. John 17:21.
13. 2 Peter 1:4.
14. cf. Colossians 3:10.
15. cf. 2 Corinthians 4:4.
16. cf. Hebrews 1:3.
17. John 17:21.

Also available in Fount Paperbacks

Silent Music
WILLIAM JOHNSTON

Silent Music is a brilliant synthesis which joins traditional religious insights with the discoveries of modern science to provide a complete picture of mysticism – its techniques and stages, its mental and physical aspects, its dangers, and its consequences.

The Inner Eye of Love
WILLIAM JOHNSTON

'This is a lucid comparison and exposition of eastern and western mysticism, from Zen to the Cloud of Unknowing, which can do nothing but good all round.'

Gerald Priestland, The Universe

The Mirror Mind
WILLIAM JOHNSTON

'William Johnston continues his first-hand studies of Zen meditation and Christian prayer . . . At his disposal he has had a twofold large and demanding literature. His use of it can be startlingly luminous.'

Bernard Lonergan

The Varieties of Religious Experience
WILLIAM JAMES

'A classic of psychological study. . . fresh and stimulating . . . this book is a book to prize.'

The Psychologist

The Religious Experience of Mankind
NINIAN SMART

'Professor Smart's patient, clear and dispassionate exposition makes him a tireless and faithful guide.'

Evening News

The Diary of a Country Priest
GEORGES BERNANOS

A famous and much admired work, the diary of 'M. Le Curé' consists in his own words of 'the very simple trivial secrets of a very ordinary life'. His manifold activities as a parish priest – all this is set down with simplicity and without guile, and the result is a moving, sincere and poignant portrait of one who is called to serve God.

Peter Abelard
HELEN WADDELL

'There are few novels of which one wonders whether one might not properly employ the word masterpiece to describe them, and this is one of them.'

The Guardian

Incognito
PETRU DUMITRIU

'Here is a novel on the grand scale – a story, grim yet compassionate . . . developed with enormous skill and acute observation through nearly 500 absorbing pages.'

The Evening Standard

Also available in Fount Paperbacks

The Sacrament of the Present Moment
JEAN-PIERRE DE CAUSSADE

'It is good to have this classic from the days of the Quietist tensions with its thesis that we can and must find God in the totality of our immediate situation . . .'

The Expository Times

The Poems of St John of the Cross
TRANSLATED BY ROY CAMPBELL

'Mr Campbell has recreated the extraordinary subtlety of the music of the original in an English verse worthy of it and that climbs from aspiration to ecstasy as if it were itself the poem.'

The Guardian

Thérèse of Lisieux
MICHAEL HOLLINGS

A superb portrait of one of the most popular of all saints.

'This book is well worth recommending . . . presents a simple factual outline of Thérèse's life and teaching . . . (with) incidents . . . applied to our own everyday lives.'

Review for Contemplatives of all Traditions

I, Francis
CARLO CARRETTO

This unusual and compelling book is a sustained meditation on the spirituality of St Francis of Assisi, bringing the meaning of his message to our time.

'A book one will not forget.'

Eric Doyle, The Tablet

Also available in Fount Paperbacks

BOOKS BY DAVID KOSSOFF

Bible Stories

'To my mind there is no doubt that these stories make the Bible come alive. Mr Kossoff is a born storyteller. He has the gift of making the old stories new.'

William Barclay

The Book of Witnesses

'The little stories are fascinating in the warm humanity they reveal. Right from the first one the reader is enthralled . . . bringing the drama of the New Testament into our daily lives with truly shattering impact.'

Religious Book News

The Voices of Masada

'This is imaginative historical writing of the highest standard.'

Church Times

The Little Book of Sylvanus

Sylvanus, the quiet, observant man, tells his version of the events surrounding the 'carpenter preacher' of Nazareth, from the Crucifixion to Pentecost. A moving and unforgettable view of the gospel story, and a sequel to *The Book of Witnesses*.

Also available in Fount Paperbacks

Audacity to Believe
SHEILA CASSIDY

'A story of extraordinarily unpretentious courage in the horror of Chile after Allende's overthrow. It is easy to read, totally sincere and sometimes moving. Sheila Cassidy is totally disarming.'

Frank O'Reilly
The Furrow

Prayer for Pilgrims
SHEILA CASSIDY

'... a direct and practical book about prayer ... has the freshness of someone who writes of what she has personally discovered ... many people ... will be grateful for this book and helped by it.'

Neville Ward
Church Times

The General Next to God
RICHARD COLLIER

'An absorbing, sympathetic record of the man (General Booth) and his family and the movement they created.'

Michael Foot
Evening Standard

Fount Paperbacks

Fount is one of the leading paperback publishers of religious books and below are some of its recent titles.

- ☐ THE QUIET HEART George Appleton £2.95
- ☐ PRAYER FOR ALL TIMES Pierre Charles £1.75
- ☐ SEEKING GOD Esther de Waal £1.75
- ☐ THE SCARLET AND THE BLACK
  J. P. Gallagher £1.75
- ☐ TELL MY PEOPLE I LOVE THEM
  Clifford Hill £1.50
- ☐ CONVERSATIONS WITH THE CRUCIFIED
  Reid Isaac £1.50
- ☐ THE LITTLE BOOK OF SYLVANUS
  David Kossoff £1.50
- ☐ DOES GOD EXIST? Hans Küng £5.95
- ☐ GEORGE MACDONALD: AN ANTHOLOGY
  George MacDonald C. S. Lewis (ed.) £1.50
- ☐ WHY I AM STILL A CATHOLIC
  Robert Nowell (ed.) £1.50
- ☐ THE GOSPEL FROM OUTER SPACE
  Robert L. Short £1.50
- ☐ CONTINUALLY AWARE Rita Snowden £1.75
- ☐ TRUE RESURRECTION Harry Williams £1.75
- ☐ WHO WILL DELIVER US? Paul Zahl £1.50

All Fount paperbacks are available at your bookshop or newsagent, or they can also be ordered by post from Fount Paperbacks, Cash Sales Department, G.P.O. Box 29, Douglas, Isle of Man, British Isles. Please send purchase price, plus 15p per book, maximum postage £3. Customers outside the U.K. send purchase price, plus 15p per book. Cheque, postal or money order. No currency.

NAME (Block letters) _____

ADDRESS _____

_____

_____